Howell Book House
A Simon & Schuster Macmillan Company
1633 Broadway
New York, NY 10019

MACMILLAN is a registered trademark of Macmillan, Inc.
Library of Congress Cataloging-in-Publication Data is available from the Library of Congress upon request.

Manufactured in the United States of America
10 9 8 7 6 5 4 3

Series Director: Dominique DeVito
Series Assistant Director: Ariel Cannon
Book Design: Michele Laseau
Cover Design: Iris Jeromnimon
Illustration: Casey Price and Jeff Yesh
Photography:
  Front cover and puppy by Paulette Braun/Pets by Paulette
  Back cover photo by Jean Wentworth
  Courtesy American Kennel Club: 14 (bottom)
  Joan Balzarini: 96
  Mary Bloom: 96, 136, 145
  Paulette Braun/Pets by Paulette: 5, 7, 8, 20, 21, 22, 23, 42, 61, 67, 90, 96
  Buckinghamhill American Cocker Spaniels: 148
  Sian Cox: 134
  Dr. Ian Dunbar: 98, 101, 103, 111, 116–117, 122, 123, 127
  Dan Lyons: 45, 96
  Cathy Merrithew: 129
  Blackie Nygood: 12, 26, 44, 55
  Liz Palika: 133
  Cheryl Primeau: 54
  Susan Rezy: 96–97
  Don Smith: 62, 64, 65, 66, 83
  Judith Strom: 14 (top), 16, 39, 68, 96, 107, 110, 128, 130, 135, 137, 139, 140, 144, 149, 150
  Faith Uridel: 2-3, 10, 32-33, 50, 69
  Jean Wentworth: 17, 27, 41, 87
Production Team: John Carroll, Kathleen Caulfield, Christina Van Camp, and Vic Peterson

Contents

Welcome to the
World
of the

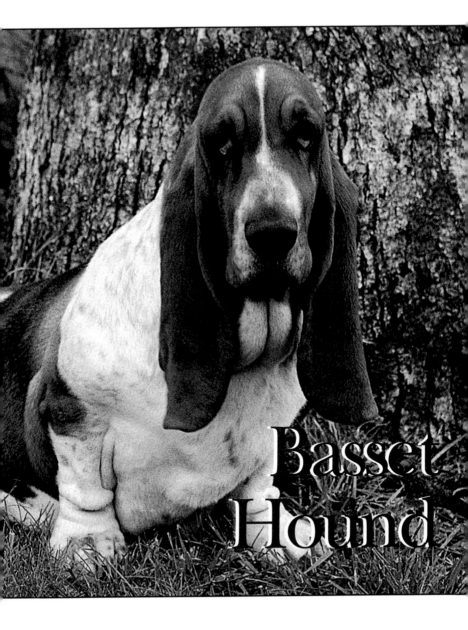

part one

Basset
Hound

External Features of the Basset Hound

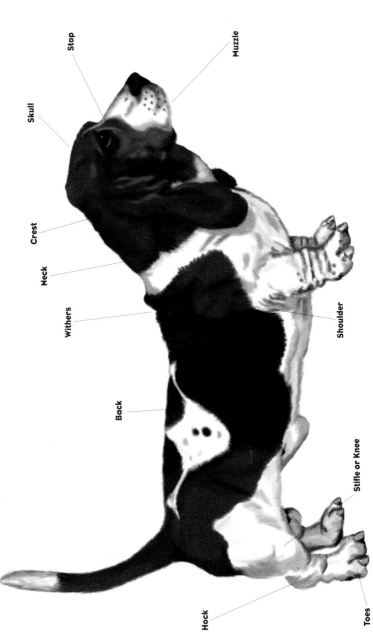

Skull

Stop

Muzzle

Crest

Neck

Withers

Shoulder

Back

Stifle or Knee

Hock

Toes

chapter 1

What
Is a
Basset Hound?

The Basset Hound: Avid hunter or couch potato? Melancholy or joyful? Playful or dormant? A picture of dignity or avowed clown?

If you share your home with a Basset Hound, you already know that your pet is all of the above. The Basset Hound's looks belie its personality at almost every turn. Often called "the clown of the dog world," the Basset's greatest joy comes in making family and friends laugh—unless, of course, he's engaged in another favorite pursuit, like snoozing on the couch or following his nose in pursuit of a rabbit.

As with most "working" breeds, the Basset Hound's form relates directly to its function, although that form will differ to some extent from one dog to another. However, certain physical characteristics combine to define a dog as a Basset Hound.

A Scent Hound

An adept hunter, the Basset Hound is part of that category of dogs known as "scent hounds," hounds who hunt by using their sense of smell rather than their vision. The Basset Hound nose is among the keenest of all breeds'—perhaps *the* keenest—enabling him to easily follow the scent of a rabbit or other quarry. The short legs are no deterrent to the Basset Hound's agility. Despite their strange build, these hounds are capable of following a rabbit over all terrain, through thick brush, over logs and through streams (although they may tackle that last obstacle with some reluctance).

The AKC Standard

The Basset Hound is built to perform a specific task with optimum efficiency, and his appearance relates directly to his assignment. Designed as a low-slung trailing hound, the Basset Hound should possess great physical stamina in order to carry out his job in the field. Exaggeration of any of the typical Basset Hound characteristics can destroy the dog's performance in the field and therefore should be avoided.

With the breed's origins and traditional activities in mind, The Basset Hound Club of America drew up the first standard for the Basset in this country. The American Kennel Club (AKC) ratified this standard in 1964, and it has served since then as the blueprint for the Basset Hound's appearance.

Ideally, every Basset Hound should live up to the standard of excellence adopted by the Basset Hound Club of America and approved by

WHAT IS A BREED STANDARD?

A breed standard—a detailed description of an individual breed—is meant to portray the *ideal* specimen of that breed. This includes ideal structure, temperament, gait, type—all aspects of the dog. Because the standard describes an ideal specimen, it isn't based on any particular dog. It is a concept against which judges compare actual dogs and breeders strive to produce dogs. At a dog show, the dog that wins is the one that comes closest, in the judge's opinion, to the standard for its breed. Breed standards are written by the breed parent clubs, the national organizations formed to oversee the well-being of the breed. They are voted on and approved by the members of the parent clubs.

the American Kennel Club. This is the description of the "perfect" Basset Hound, and those competing in the show ring are measured against the standard. In the discussion below, italicized text is the official standard; the author's commentary follows in regular text. (For a complete copy of the Basset Hound Standard, contact the American Kennel Club. See Chapter 13, "Resources," for the address.)

General Appearance

The Basset Hound . . . is a short-legged dog, heavier in bone, size considered, than any other breed of dog, and while its movement is deliberate, it is in no sense clumsy. In temperament it is mild, never sharp or timid. It is capable of endurance in the field and is extreme in its devotion.

Although the standard does not specify the exact dimensions of the ideal Basset Hound, most breeders would agree that the height at the withers should be about three-fourths of the length from withers to tail. Those who tend to think of the Basset Hound as a "small" dog should reread the section above: "heavier in bone, size considered, than any other breed of dog." In reality, the Basset Hound is a large dog on short legs, typically weighing anywhere from fifty to seventy pounds.

The wrinkles on the Basset Hound's head help him trap and follow the scent of prey.

HEAD

*The head is large and well proportioned. Its length from occiput to muzzle is greater than the width at the brow. In over-all appearence the head is of medium width. The **skull** is well domed, showing a pronounced occipital protuberance. The sides are flat and free of cheek bumps. Viewed in profile the top lines of the muzzle and skull are straight and lie in parallel planes, with a moderately defined stop. The skin over* *the whole of the head is loose, falling in distinct wrinkles over the brow when the head is lowered.*

The Basset Hound head should be large and well proportioned, of medium width with a well-domed skull showing a "pronounced occipital protuberance." When the head is lowered, loose, distinct wrinkles should be evident over the brow. The elasticity and wrinkles help protect the Basset Hound's skin from puncture wounds during field work. It is theorized that these folds of skin may also help the dog detect the scent of the prey.

Long, velvety ears are a hallmark of the Basset Hound.

The nose itself should be black, although a liver-colored nose is permissible if it conforms to the color of the dog's head. The teeth should be large and regular, and the jaws should meet in either a scissors or an even bite. An overshot or undershot bite is considered a serious fault in the show ring, although it is not likely to interfere with a pet's appetite or ability to chow down.

*The **lips** are darkly pigmented and are pendulous, falling squarely in front and toward the back, in loose hanging flews. The **dewlap** is very pronounced. The **neck** is powerful, of good length and well arched.*

The neck is particularly important to the Basset Hound's ability to hunt. It should be sufficiently long to allow the nose comfortably to reach the ground and do its work. Too short a neck can strain the dog, thus impeding its progress in the field.

*The **eyes** should be soft, sad, and slightly sunken, showing a prominent haw, and in color are brown, preferably dark brown. A somewhat lighter colored eye conforming to the general coloring of the dog is acceptable but not desirable. Very light or protruding eyes are considered show ring faults.*

Without those spectacular "puppy dog eyes" the Basset would not be half as charming.

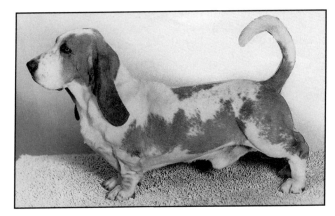

Though his legs are short, the Basset Hound cannot be considered a small dog.

*The **ears** are extremely long, low set, and when drawn forward fold well over the end of the nose. They are velvety in texture, hanging in loose folds with the ends curling slightly inward. They are set far back on the head at the base of the skull, and, in repose, appear to be set on the neck. A high set or flat ear is a serious flaw.*

The ears are the hallmark of the Basset Hound's appearance. However, though an integral part of the breed's appearance, long ears should not be exaggerated. The ears serve a valuable function in stirring up the scent in the field, but they should not be so long as to interfere with the dog's work.

BODY

*The **chest** is deep and full with a prominent sternum showing clearly on the front of the legs.*

A chest of this style and fortitude gives the Basset Hound the stamina necessary for a full day's work.

Shoulders *and elbows are set close against the sides of the chest. The distance from the deepest point of the chest to the*

ground, while it must be adequate to allow free movement when working in the field, should not be more than one-third the height at the withers of an adult Basset Hound.

The Basset was bred to work long hours in the field, and must be an efficent mover and a hearty companion. This conformation helps the Basset Hound move with the utmost efficiency.

Shoulders are well laid back and powerful. The **forelegs** *are short, powerful and heavy boned, covered with wrinkled skin. The* **paw** *is massive, well rounded, and very heavy with tough, thick pads. Both feet should be inclined equally a trifle outward, balancing the width of the shoulders. The toes are neither pinched together nor splayed, with the weight. The ribs structure is long, smooth, and extends well back . . . allowing adequate room for the heart and lungs. The topline is straight, level and free from any tendency to sag or roach.*

The color and distribution of markings on a Basset are of no consequence.

A rib cage of proper length provides support for the lumbar vertebrae, thus minimizing the possibility of the dog developing back problems.

The Basset Hound also requires strong hindquarters to propel its heavy body through the field. Thus, the standard calls for *hindquarters to be very full and well-rounded, approximately equal to the shoulders in width. Viewed from behind, the hind legs are parallel, with the hocks pointing neither in nor out.* An "apple-round rear" is the phrase most often used to describe the ideal Basset Hound hindquarters. The tail is an extension of the spine with a slight curve, and "should be carried gaily in hound fashion." The tail is the Basset Hound's "flag," signaling the dog's location when working in heavy underbrush. Although most Basset Hounds have a white tip on the tail, making it easier to follow them in the field, the standard does not require this.

SIZE

The height should not exceed 14 inches. Height over 15 inches at the highest point of the shoulder blades is a disqualification.

The average Basset Hound stands between twelve and a half and thirteen and a half inches at the withers (shoulders), and those standing more than fifteen inches are to be disqualified from the show ring.

GAIT

The Basset Hound moves in a smooth, powerful, and effortless manner. Being a scenting dog with short legs, it holds its nose close to the ground.

Although the Basset Hound may at first seem clumsy, it should move in a smooth, powerful and effortless manner. Front and hind legs should be perfectly coordinated as the Basset Hound moves in deliberate, determined fashion.

COAT

The coat is hard, smooth and short, with sufficient density to be of use in all weather. The skin is loose and elastic.

THE AMERICAN KENNEL CLUB

Familiarly referred to as "the AKC," the American Kennel Club is a nonprofit organization devoted to the advancement of purebred dogs. The AKC maintains a registry of recognized breeds and adopts and enforces rules for dog events including shows, obedience trials, field trials, hunting tests, lure coursing, herding, earthdog trials, agility and the Canine Good Citizen program. It is a club of clubs, established in 1884 and composed, today, of over 500 autonomous dog clubs throughout the United States. Each club is represented by a delegate; the delegates make up the legislative body of the AKC, voting on rules and electing directors. The American Kennel Club maintains the Stud Book, the record of every dog ever registered with the AKC, and publishes a variety of materials on purebred dogs, including a monthly magazine, books and numerous educational pamphlets. For more information, contact the AKC at the address listed in Chapter 13, "Resources," and look for the names of their publications in Chapter 12, "Recommended Reading."

The Basset Hound's loose skin renders him "punctureproof" in the field. The coarse, thick coat protects him from any weather. Any recognized hound color is acceptable, and distribution of color and markings is of no consequence. Recognized hound colors are black, brown and white, the shades of brown ranging from mahogany to lemon. Lemon is the palest color seen in Bassets, with red somewhere in the middle. Red and white and lemon and white Bassets usually display no black.

It doesn't matter if your pet Basset Hound lives up to all the requirements of the standard; she will still be a loving member of the family.

Disqualifications

The Basset Hound standard contains three show ring disqualifications: height over fifteen inches at the shoulder, knuckled-over front legs and a distinctly long coat. These disqualifications do not apply to dogs entered in field trials, obedience trials, tracking tests or agility tests, so a dog who is not up to snuff for the show ring is nevertheless eligible to compete in American Kennel Club performance events. Spayed or neutered dogs may not participate in the show ring or in field trials, but may compete in any of the other AKC activities listed here. (See chapter 9 for additional information about organized activities for your dog.)

A versatile breed, the Basset Hound is capable of participating in and enjoying a wide variety of activities. Take advantage of this aspect of the breed, and don't despair if your pet fails to meet every specification of the standard. In fact, no one has yet come up with the perfect dog of any breed. The important thing is that someone admiring your pet can look at him, recognize him for what he is and remark, "What a lovely Basset Hound!"

The
Basset Hound's
Ancestry

Figures of a dog with the same proportions as the Basset Hound have been found on an Egyptian monument erected earlier than 2000 BC. Early Assyrian dog sculptures also display Basset Hound–like features. However, though ancestors of the Basset may have existed in one form or  another in these ancient civilizations, it was the French who developed this breed into the small scent hound we know today.

The French Origins

The Basset Hound originated in France, and for a very specific purpose. The expectation was that this "dwarf" breed would be able to follow game animals at a slower pace than other hounds, thus allowing the hunters to trail their quarry and dogs without riding horseback. The short legs would also allow the Basset Hound to keep its nose close to the ground through heavy brush without tiring. The French were not disappointed, as this new hunting hound carried out their intent with the greatest success.

The word basset means low-set in French, a perfect description of the Basset Hound.

There is more than one theory about the origin of the Basset Hound in France. The most accepted is that the breed descended from the St. Hubert's Hound, but Mercedes Braun, author of *The Complete Basset Hound* (Howell Book House, 1979), believes that its ancestor is the Basset Artesien Normand, once known in France as the Basset d'Artois.

Basset Hounds are still used to track rabbits today.

Traditionally, the French named all breeds shorter than sixteen inches "Basset." The word *bas* means low-set in French; and *basset*, along with other descriptive words, was included in the name of a large variety of provincial breeds.

English Influence

Although there is evidence of the short-legged hounds in France probably as early as the 1500s, the first imports didn't find their way to England until 1880.

From this breeding stock developed the heavier boned dog with the Bloodhound-type head we know today. There has been speculation that the Basset of St. Hubert entered the picture in England in order to help develop some of the physical characteristics of the modern-day Basset Hound.

This depiction of a Basset Hound appeared in The Illustrated Sporting and Dramatic News *in 1884.*

In 1894 British breeder Sir Everett Millais, apparently dissatisfied with the effects if inbreeding on his Basset Hounds, used artificial insemination to crossbreed a Basset Hound dog to a Bloodhound bitch. The Basset Hound anatomy prevailed through the crossbreeding, and although that first litter was uniformly Bloodhound color (black and tan), follow-up breedings with these puppies produced tricolors and gave Sir Edward what he was looking for: larger, healthier hounds.

Hunting with Basset Hound packs gained popularity in England, and later extended to the United States, where the hare or rabbit is hunted in its natural habitat with a pack of at least ten hounds. St. Hubert is the patron saint of the hunt, and a "Blessing of the Hunt" takes place on or close to St. Hubert's Day in early November.

FAMOUS OWNERS OF BASSET HOUND

Peter Falk

Clint Eastwood

Rex Harrison

Bob Hope

Arthur Milller and Marilyn Monroe

George Washington

The Basset Hound in the United States

The first recorded data about the Basset Hound coming to America supposedly appears in George

Washington's diaries. His friend, the French general Lafayette, sent hounds to General Washington after the Revolutionary War. Lord Aylesford brought a brace (pair of hounds) to his Big Springs, Texas, ranch for rabbit hunting in 1883, the same year an English show dog, Nemours, was sent to New Jersey.

George Washington's Bassets were brought to the United States to track rabbits, just as this modern Basset is doing.

Nemours made his show ring debut in this country in the spring of 1884 at the Westminster Kennel Club show, introducing this new breed to the American public who responded enthusiastically. In 1935 the Basset Hound Club of America was formed, though it wasn't until 1937 that the club held the first Basset Hound field trial in this country. Many of the dogs of this era competed both in the field and in the show ring. They were truly versatile, dual-purpose dogs.

A Basset Hound Relative

Among the French *basset* breeds is another currently gaining popularity in the United States that, "though a cousin to the Basset Hound, should not be mistaken for a variety of the same breed." The Petit Basset Griffon Vendeen (which originated in the Vendée region of France), is a wire-coated (griffon), smaller, almost terrierlike hound, somewhat higher on leg and shorter in body than the Basset Hound. The uninitiated frequently think of the PBGV as a wire-coated Basset Hound, but this is inaccurate at best. Although the PBGV's function is similar to the Basset Hound's, its attitude is not. It is an extremely active and playful breed, and a pet owner who wants a relaxed, laid-back dog should stick with the Basset Hound. Though the PBGV certainly has its charm, it should be left to those who enjoy perpetual motion.

Depictions of the Basset Hound

Although William Shakespeare's writings contain some decidedly derogatory references to dogs, *A Midsummer Night's Dream* contains these lines:

> *My hounds are bred out of the Spartan kind,*
>
> *So flew'd, so sanded, and their heads are hung*
>
> *With ears that sweep away the morning dew;*
>
> *Crook-knee'd and dew-lapp'd like Thessalian bulls;*
>
> *Slow in pursuit, but match'd in mouth like bells;*
>
> *Each under each.*

If these lines were not intended to be descriptive of the Basset Hound, they come as close to it as is possible.

It's easy to see why the Basset Hound lends itself to humorous depictions.

Basset Hounds appear in French paintings dating to the mid-1800s. There are numerous fine sculptures of Basset Hounds, including one that is on display in the library of the American Kennel Club, donated by the Basset Hound Club of America.

In addition to the serious literature written about Basset Hounds, several children's books as well as

17

adult humor books have used the breed as a popular model.

That the breed lends itself to humor is evidenced by its presence in the comics and on television. The Basset Hound's acceptance and popularity soared in the 1960s when the television series *The People's Choice*, starring Jackie Cooper and Cleo the Basset, captivated viewers. Cleo's frequent public appearances at pet-related events made new friends for the Basset Hound, and that popularity has continued to grow.

Many who are too young to remember Cleo were drawn to the breed through the comic-page antics of *Fred Basset*, whose creator, A. Graham, clearly has had a wealth of experience with this lovable clown of the dog world. More recently, the dog Quincy has graced the small screen with an occasional appearance in the series *Coach*.

Peter Falk, star of the television detective series *Colombo*, is an avid Basset Hound enthusiast and has lent his support to fund-raising efforts in California on behalf of homeless Basset Hounds. Former professional football running back Mike Garrett is also an unabashed fan of the breed, and although his travel schedule while playing was not conducive to dog ownership, he "adopted" a bitch owned by a friend and was photographed with her.

The Basset Hound has also been associated with the popular products Maytag appliances and Hush Puppies shoes. The common appearance of these spokesbassets has made the breed increasingly familiar. After all, who could resist such a face?

English royalty in the nineteenth century was enamored of this unique breed as well, so you can be assured that you're not the "odd person out" because you've chosen a Basset Hound to share your life.

chapter 3

The **World**
According to the
Basset Hound

The Basset Hound was bred to follow the scent of a rabbit or hare along the ground, to pursue his quarry single-mindedly. For this purpose, early Basset breeders chose stock that fit their blueprint for both a dedicated and focused personality, and a strong, low-slung physique. The Basset Hound's good temper has made it a popular breed today when a dog is much more likely to be the family pet than the family hunter. Basset Hounds today are both strong scent hounds and loving companions. You will also find, as your relationship with your Basset develops, that each individual Basset has a personality all his own.

An Independent Dog

The Basset Hound's function as a scent hound is responsible for many of the breed's personality characteristics, primarily its independence. There is little we humans can do to assist the Basset Hound (or any scent hound) in carrying out its mission to hunt by using its sharp sense of smell. Independence is a natural characteristic of the Basset Hound and its cousins, who rely on their noses to do their jobs.

The Basset Hound's independent streak often tends to be misunderstood, and may be defined as stubbornness or, by the truly uninitiated, as stupidity. Stubborn, yes. Stupid, never!

Bred to hunt single-mindedly with his nose, the Basset Hound has an independent personality.

Most Basset Hounds are quite capable of outsmarting their owners at almost every turn, and take great delight in doing just that. That does not mean they're incapable of learning what you want them to learn. It merely means that they will learn it on *their* terms rather than yours.

Obedience for Bassets?

Many consider Basset Hounds to be inappropriate dogs for obedience competition. Indeed, for the serious, score-conscious competitor, there are more suitable breeds. A Basset Hound can be an absolute embarrassment, not due to lack of intelligence or learning ability but because he's determined to learn by *his* rules. Equally strong is the Basset Hound's unerring mission to entertain and amuse at every opportunity.

Perhaps the most repeated Basset Hound obedience story—and one that is true—concerns a dog named George. He achieved his companion dog (CD) and companion dog excellent (CDX) titles, but hit a major snag when working towards his utility dog (UD) title. George learned quickly that he could become the center of attention and get lots of laughs if, instead of bringing back the glove on command, he returned to his owner with his *ear* in his mouth. Once George devised this trick there was no unlearning it. He kept it up until his frustrated owner retired him from competition and switched to an easier, less creative breed. (For more information on obedience and other activities for you and your dog, see chapter 9.)

Patient training is necessary to make your Basset a happy and well-behaved pet.

The Basset Hound's nose also has been known to create problems in the obedience ring. There are numerous stories about Bassets leaving the obedience ring to befriend a spectator eating a hot dog at ringside. One of my own hounds left the ring at her first opportunity during competition at a national specialty to check out the nearby refreshment stand.

Bassets Need Training

This is not to say that the Basset Hound can't do its owner proud in the obedience ring. It can, and many have. However, the training techniques must be compatible with the Basset Hound temperament, and it helps if you can convince your dog the whole silly thing was *his* idea to begin with! Treats and praise work wonders; punishment and heavy-handedness can bring about a total shutdown of response. Although the Basset Hound can be as tough as any breed while doing its work in the field, it also is extremely sensitive and rarely tolerates harsh treatment. (See chapter 8 for basic training information.)

Patience and perseverance will help a Basset Hound owner survive the training and adjustment period with a new pet. One key to success is establishing early on who is leading the pack known as the family. Never, under any circumstances, should the dog be the leader! Too often owners of a cute little Basset Hound puppy (and they are the cutest pups) will let the four-legged youngster get away with all kinds of shenanigans until it's too late.

"He's just a puppy; I can't discipline him. Besides, he's so cute," you may insist. Wrong. If the discipline doesn't start from day one, you'll soon find that your cute puppy has become overbearing and unbearable. He'll do only what *he* wants to do, and may resort to aggression when you decide to take charge. By this time, he's no longer a small puppy but has matured into a large, strong dog.

Bassets can be successful in organized activities, such as obedience, with the right training and encouragement.

Don't be fooled by the short legs. By no stretch of the imagination is the Basset Hound a small dog. Heavier in bone for its size than any other breed, the male Basset Hound can weigh up to seventy-plus pounds, and the female up to fifty-five or sixty pounds. This can be a lot of uncontrollable dog. To the size and strength add the low-slung physique, which gives the dog a low center of gravity, plus the stubborn nature of the breed, and you'll have a major problem on your hands unless you get off to a good start with your pet.

Friendly and Good-Natured

Bassets are great family pets, and tend to love all the members of the family equally. They are good with children, provided of course that both the children

23

and the Basset have enough discipline to treat the other properly. Bassets were bred to hunt in a pack, and are not single-person dogs. They love everyone and are quite demonstrative with their affections.

The Basset Hound temperament, according to the standard of excellence, should be "mild, never timid or sharp." Indeed, those Basset Hounds who receive proper upbringing, both in the whelping box and in their new homes, will live up to that section of the standard and rarely give their owners any fear. When temperament problems do develop, they usually can be traced to the puppy being removed from its littermates and dam at too early an age—responsible breeders won't let their puppies go until at least seven or eight weeks of age—or to a home environment that either is too permissive or too severe. Heredity also can be a factor in poor temperament, but responsible, reputable breeders do not use ill-tempered dogs as breeding stock, and the problems that crop up among Basset Hounds are usually environmental.

CHARACTERISTICS OF THE BASSET HOUND

Independent

Friendly

Loves Children

Stubborn

Clownish

Tends to drool

Does not require lots of exercise

By remaining with his littermates and mother during those early, formative weeks, a puppy becomes socialized and gains the rudiments of discipline. Those lessons, however, must not end when the puppy goes off to his new home. Training and discipline must continue if the Basset Hound is to develop into the mild-mannered dog he should be.

Harsh discipline, however, is rarely called for or required. A stern "no" accompanied by a brief shaking of the dog by the collar, with front feet off the floor, should get the message across to a puppy that his behavior is unacceptable. After all, this is the disciplinary method used by his mother in the whelping box.

With some breeds, one or two such corrections probably will suffice. With a Basset Hound, be prepared to exert as much determination as does your dog for how-ever long it may take. But take heart. The day will come when your Basset Hound decides he's lost this battle and it's time to give in to your whims. The timely use of extra special treats will help hasten the surrender process.

Through training, the owner can set the tone for the kind of behavior to be expected from the Basset Hound, but there are some characteristics unique to the breed over which we have little control. The Basset Hound is not the ideal pet for finicky housekeepers, allergy sufferers or those with very sensitive noses. Nothing smells quite so fragrant as a wet hound, com-ing indoors and rolling around on the carpeting to dry off!

Bassets Bark

Basset Hounds working in the field are *required* to "give tongue" as they chase their quarry, and this original function has produced a breed that is often noisy. Although some Bassets are relatively quiet, most of them are not suitable apartment dogs unless the owner is prepared to do some serious training.

. . . And They Can Be Messy

There are ways of minimizing the less endearing qual-ities of the Basset Hound. Though the Basset Hound, being a hound, may impart a particularly "doggy" odor, this can be controlled. Nonchemical "odor-eaters" are available in most good pet supply stores, and these can be used in your washing machine when doing the dog's bedding (frequently), and even in the rinse water when bathing the dog. Proper use of such prod-ucts will help reduce the hound odor.

The Basset Hound's heavy "flews" (lips) make this one of the breeds that tends to slobber, or drool. Though females usually have drier mouths than males, they too can project that drool to the ceiling with little effort. Also, the typically oily coat that serves the Basset Hound so well in the field will leave ugly dirt marks on the walls where your hound leans or rubs. The simplest solution to the slobber and dirt problems is the use of washable paint or other easy-to-clean wall surfaces in those rooms accessible to your Basset Hound.

If you've decided that your pet is welcome on your sofa, you should provide a throw cover for the dog to lie on rather than letting the hound odor and drool permeate the fabric. If, however, your pet scrunches up the cover and ends up on the couch proper, there are several reliable cleaning products available in pet supply stores that are effective in getting rid of pet odors and stains.

Like all breeds, the Basset Hound thrives on giving and receiving affection.

For the accident-prone puppy who's still in the house-training stage, it's a good idea to keep on hand one of those products designed to eliminate urine and feces odors. Remember, the Basset Hound's keen nose (even as a puppy) will bring him back to the same spot unless you thoroughly eliminate the smell.

Other sources of odor can be the skin, teeth and ears. The wrinkles can cause skin problems, and the heavy, long ears become easily infected unless maintained on a regular basis. Tartar buildup on the teeth leads to bad breath and infection. Monitor your pet's skin and coat so any problems that arise can be brought under quick control with the help of your veterinarian. Pay close attention to the areas under the chin, on the throat, on the tops of the feet and under the armpits, where the skin folds tend to encourage "hot spots." Clean ears regularly to prevent infection and foul odor (see chapter 6 for complete information).

A Social Dog

Though the Basset Hound may require some management as a housepet, keeping him as an outside dog probably will present even more serious problems, most of them insurmountable. Basically a social being, the Basset Hound does not take well to being isolated from the family, either on a tie-out or in a pen, for any long period of time. The dog's reaction to such banishment frequently is to howl, loudly and persistently,

You will need to make sure your backyard or exercise area is firmly enclosed; Bassets have a tendency to follow their noses right out of the yard.

raising the hackles of neighbors who are, after all, entitled to some peace and quiet. More than one owner of an "outside" Basset Hound has called for advice on how to deal with this problem or, in desperation, for help in getting rid of the dog.

"He's quiet until we go out in the yard. Then he starts to bark and howl," is a frequent gripe. "We want to be able to enjoy our yard without the neighbors complaining." The reason for the dog's behavior is simple: He craves attention. Once he spots his people, he wants to join the group and not remain isolated in a corner of the yard.

The Escape Artist

The outside Basset Hound also is apt to disappear at some point, and may never return. Most Bassets can work themselves free by slipping the collar, by chewing whatever is holding them tethered or by digging under a fence. People are always amazed at how far and how fast a Basset Hound can travel, again being fooled by those short legs and overlooking the scent hound determination and instinct to follow a trail, no matter how far it leads.

We once found a young Basset Hound running loose alongside a major highway, picked him up and advertised in the lost-and-found section of the area newspaper for his owner. She responded, and was astonished that he had traveled three or four miles from home. Of course, his return would have been facilitated had he been wearing a collar with an identification tag.

Although it's easier to keep up with a running Basset Hound than with a "coursing" hound, such as the Greyhound, Bassets can be remarkably difficult to catch. While the hound nose probably can help your pet find his way home again, the Basset Hound typically shows no fear of traffic and thus no common sense in dealing with it. Indeed, Bassets have been known to take a nap in the middle of a roadway if they tire of the chase and decide to take a break. To keep your dog alive and safe, keep him confined or on a leash at all times. It takes only a split second, and an amazingly small opening, for a Basset Hound to scoot out an open door or under a fence and be gone. Children and visitors to the household should be watched

---

A DOG'S SENSES

Sight: With their eyes located farther apart than ours, dogs can detect movement at a greater distance than we can, but they can't see as well up close. They can also see better in less light, but can't distinguish many colors.

Sound: Dogs can hear about four times better than we can, and they can hear high-pitched sounds especially well. Their ancestors, the wolves, howled to let other wolves know where they were; our dogs do the same, but they have a wider range of vocalizations, including barks, whimpers, moans and whines.

Smell: A dog's nose is his greatest sensory organ. His sense of smell is so great he can follow a trail that's weeks old, detect odors diluted to one-millionth the concentration we'd need to notice them, even sniff out a person under water!

Taste: Dogs have fewer taste buds than we do, so they're likelier to try anything—and usually do, which is why it's especially important for their owners to monitor their food intake. Dogs are omnivores, which means they eat meat as well as vegetable matter like grasses and weeds.

Touch: Dogs are social animals and love to be petted, groomed and played with.

carefully to make sure doors and fence gates are not left open or held ajar while a departing guest stops to engage in one last bit of conversation.

Your Basset's Back

If your pet, with your blessing, is a "couch potato," you should be aware of the potential for injury. Climbing up on the furniture usually is not a problem, but jumping down off a couch or bed puts a great deal of pressure on the Basset Hound spine and could lead to serious injury. It's a good idea to train your Basset Hound to wait for assistance in getting down from the furniture in order to prevent spinal trauma. We also always teach our hounds to wait for help getting in and out of cars. Our dogs get their front feet up and then wait for a boost from the rear as a precaution against back injuries.

Understanding the nature of the Basset Hound's personality and physique—and the functional reasons why he is what he is—will go a long way toward helping you live with your pet, and will contribute greatly to your appreciation and enjoyment of him.

MORE INFORMATION ON BASSET HOUNDS

NATIONAL BREED CLUB

Basset Hound Club of America, Inc.
Melody Fair, Corresponding Secretary
P.O. Box 339
Noti, OR 97461

The club secretary can provide you with breed information, an application for membership and referral to a breed club in your own area.

BOOKS

Braun, Mercedes. *The New Complete Basset Hound.* New York: Howell Book House, 1979.

Foy, Marcia, and Anna Katherine Nicholas. *The Basset Hound.* New Jersey: THF Publications, 1985.

Walton, Margaret S. *The New Basset Hound.* New York: Howell Book House, 1993.

MAGAZINES

Tally-Ho, published five times a year by the Basset Hound Club of America, Inc., for its members. Contains educational materials as well as news about club activities.

The Bugler, published monthly, with lots of good information for the pet owner and show enthusiast alike. P.O. Box 698, McMinnville, TN 37110.

VIDEOS

American Kennel Club, *The Basset Hound.*

World Wide Web

Check out the following addresses on the World Wide Web for up to the minute information on Basset Hounds.

http://www.zsmall.com/pet_talk/dog_faqs/breeds/bassets.html

http://www2.uic.edu/~sschul3/b1.html

http://princeton.edu/!nedelman/bhca/bhca.html

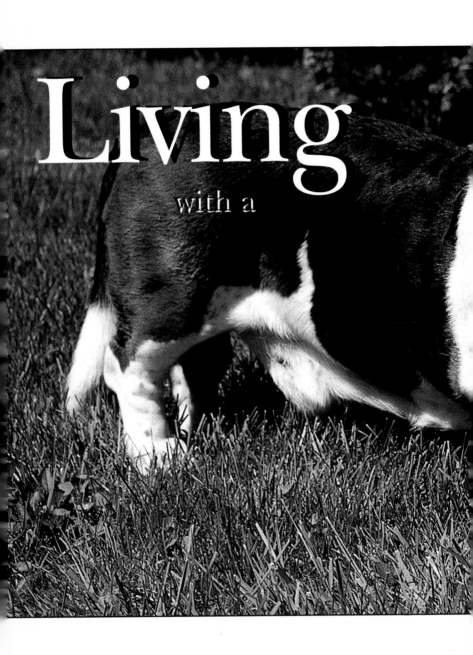

Living

with a

part two

Basset Hound

chapter 4

Bringing Your
Basset Hound
Home

Before you decide to bring a Basset Hound into your home and your life, there are some issues that must be considered carefully.

A Basset Hound in the Family

Puppies (and all pets) are a long-term, major commitment. Before bringing one into your home, the entire family must understand the responsibilities of pet ownership and must decide how those responsibilities will be shared. Children, anxious to have a dog of their own, are often quick to volunteer for duties such as feeding, walking, cleanup and grooming. Unfortunately, though their intentions may be the best, youngsters soon lose interest in these chores once the novelty wears off and other amusement opportunities surface. So, if a child is to be the primary caregiver of the new pup, be prepared for this venture to fail.

We once placed a delightful six-year-old Basset Hound whose original owners decided to give her up so they could travel. The new family kept her for two years and then returned her to us. To our horror, she was emaciated and dirty. Their excuse? "The kids were supposed to take care of her and they just wouldn't do it." The dog, of course, was the one who suffered while the children who broke their word to their naive parents went unpunished. Happily, Emmie recovered quickly and went off to still another new home, where she was loved and appreciated.

Choosing Your Basset Hound Puppy

You have read up on the Basset Hound and its idiosyncrasies, consulted with all members of the family and made sure you can fit a puppy into your life. The next step, of course, is to find that puppy you are so excited about getting. Your best bet is to buy your Basset puppy from a reputable breeder in your area. Your vet or pet shop may keep a list of local Basset Hound breeders, or you can call the Basset Hound Club of America for a recommendation. This does not mean that you can't get a great puppy from another source, but buying from a breeder has several advantages. Getting your new puppy from a reputable breeder is the best guarantee that your new puppy is a healthy, quality Basset. Also, breeders usually have many years of experience with their chosen breed, and often have more specific knowledge of common problems the breed encounters than even your vet. As a new puppy and new Basset Hound owner, your breeder will be a reliable source of advice. If you buy from a breeder, you will likely be able to see the puppies' mother, often the father or a photo of him, and perhaps even the grandparents. This will help to give you a good idea of how your puppy will look and act as he matures.

There is not much difference between male and female Bassets except their size; males are usually longer and weigh more that females. Because you will likely be spaying or neutering your Basset, this will minimize the differences between the sexes even further. Whether you prefer male or female Bassets is, therefore, largely a matter of personal taste.

Pick an outgoing, friendly puppy. Though you may feel sorry for the quiet one who lags in the corner, be aware that a timidity can develop into a poor temperament as the puppy grows.

CHOOSING A NAME

One of the first things you will need to do when you pick your puppy is to choose a name for him. Like babies, though, you don't know much about your puppy yet. You don't have much to go on except looks, so use your imagination. Just make sure it's a name that conveys your affection for your new puppy, and one that you won't be embarrassed calling out across the park.

The important thing is not to change the name once you've chosen it. This will confuse your puppy, and just lengthen the time it will take for her to start responding to you. Use her name over and over again when you praise her and speak to her; look her right in the eyes and repeat it. Don't use lots of cute nicknames to start off with. Just address her with her name in a cheerful tone of voice and she will start responding to it quickly.

Supplies

Once all members of the family are aware of the work involved and agree to shoulder their particular duties, it's time to prepare your house and property and to go shopping for supplies for the new pet. Basic purchases should include food and water dishes (stainless steel is easy to clean and durable, even under the challenge of a teething puppy); teething toys made of hard rubber or heavy-duty plastic; nail clippers; grooming supplies; a good-quality puppy food (recommended by the puppy's breeder); a dog bed, leash and collar; pooper-scoopers; an identification tag; and a crate.

Using a Crate

That last item is among the most important purchases you'll ever make for your new pet. Many pet owners have the misconception that crating a dog is cruel, but use of the crate has saved many a dog from injury and banishment. No one can watch a puppy every minute, and the dog crate is the most practical way to keep the pet out of mischief and out of harm's way. Puppy curiosity can lead to electrical wiring, toxic substances (which should be kept out of reach at all times), new shoes and a variety of other chewables. None of these temptations will cross the path of a crated puppy or dog.

In addition to safeguarding your puppy and your household belongings, the crate is a useful housetraining tool and doubles as a den for your pet when he feels the need for privacy and quiet time. The dog is, after all, a den animal, and if the crate is used properly your pet will welcome the opportunity to retreat to it.

The crate also will help you establish a training schedule, and it will keep your puppy from looking for mischief when the rest of the household is sleeping or busy with nonanimal chores.

The crate *never* should be used as punishment. Though some puppies or dogs might resist going in at first, a few well-placed treats will convince most rather quickly that this is a good place to be. The crate should be large enough to accommodate your dog comfortably, so that he can stand and turn around. It should not be so large that it can be divided into bedroom and bathroom. Most dogs will not mess where they sleep, so don't give your pet sufficient room to do both. A large crate can be "subdivided," allowing it to be lengthened as the puppy grows and requires additional footage. Be careful to select one with the bars sufficiently close together so your puppy cannot get his head caught in them.

The crate, complete with comfortable bedding and water cup, should be used when the puppy is alone or

PUPPY ESSENTIALS

Your new puppy will need:

food bowl

water bowl

collar

leash

I.D. tag

bed

crate

toys

grooming supplies

unsupervised. Immediately upon removing the puppy from the crate, take him outside. Dogs need to know when their behavior is acceptable, so when your puppy eliminates outdoors praise is in order, followed by some freedom in the home. If the puppy uses the outside time strictly for play and sniffing around, it's back in the crate for another half hour, and then repeat the routine.

The First Night

When you bring home your Basset Hound puppy, this is likely the first time she has ever been away from her mother and littermates for any long period of time. She will be a little overwhelmed, especially at first, and her first night in your home may not be the most peaceful. Put your puppy to bed in her crate with lots of soft blankets. Keep the crate in your room so she can be comforted by your closeness. Do not take her out when she starts to cry, but do offer her assuring words and let her know you are nearby. Some people suggest wrapping a ticking alarm clock in a blanket and putting it in the puppy's crate; it simulates the mother's heartbeat and calms the puppy down.

A Schedule for You and Your Puppy

One thing you can do to make your puppy happier and more secure in his new home is to establish a schedule and stick to it as much as possible. Your puppy will be happier if he knows when he will be fed and walked; what time his family will be home; when he'll be let out. When you are setting up your puppy's schedule consider

---

HOUSEHOLD DANGERS

Curious puppies and inquisitive dogs get into trouble not because they are bad, but simply because they want to investigate the world around them. It's our job to protect our dogs from harmful substances, like the following:

IN THE HOUSE

cleaners, especially pine oil

perfumes, colognes, aftershaves

medications, vitamins

office and craft supplies

electric cords

chicken or turkey bones

chocolate

some house and garden plants, like ivy, oleander and poinsettia

IN THE GARAGE

antifreeze

garden supplies, like snail and slug bait, pesticides, fertilizers, mouse and rat poisons the family's timetable: what time people are at home to play with the puppy, when family members get home from work, when they leave in the morning and what other obligations they have in the evenings. If family members usually wake up at 7 and leave the house at 8, someone will have to start waking up earlier to walk, feed and pay attention to the puppy. If people are gone during the day, is there someone who can come by and let the puppy out, feed her and play with her for a bit? (If not, it's probably better to wait to get a puppy.)

Taking your puppy on regular walks is necessary for fitness and helpful for housetraining.

Housetraining

For any dog entering a new environment, learning the household schedule is the key to housetraining. Most dogs need to go out immediately upon awakening, twenty minutes to a half hour after meals and before bedtime. Puppies, with their immature bladders, require more frequent outings. It's a good idea to rush your pup outside after a strenuous play session, since the excitement inevitably will trigger the need for a potty break.

Distinguish "exercise" walks from recreational walks so your pet knows exactly what's expected of him. Take him to the same "bathroom" spot each time, and don't embark on your recreational walk around the block until after he's eliminated and received his praise. Then you can say, "Let's go!" and take off at a brisk pace just for fun.

One new Basset Hound owner complained that he took his dog for two or three long walks a day and nothing happened until they got back in the house. Questioning him further, we discovered that this dog was being treated solely to *recreational* walks, and wasn't being given time to drop his nose to the ground to sniff out the best "bathroom" spots. We had to convince the owner to slow down and give the dog time to relieve himself *before* starting on the fun part of their walks together. (See chapter 8 for detailed house-training information.)

If you exercise your dog in your own yard, cleanup is most easily accomplished with the use of pooper-scoopers. To get rid of the odor that inevitably will build up, you can hose the yard down with bleach or any one of several products on the shelves of pet supply stores. If you lack a fenced yard and will be walking your dog on public streets, carry a pocket full of plastic baggies for pickup. More sophisticated "poop" bags can be purchased, but sandwich bags will do the job just as well. The important thing is that you are a good neighbor and don't leave a mess in your wake.

Puppyproofing

"Puppyproofing" your home and yard is an important element of successful dog ownership. Puppyproofing will protect your furniture and belongings from your curious, energetic puppy, and will also keep him safe from anything in your home or yard that could be dangerous. When you are puppyproofing, take the precautions you would for an inquisitive toddler.

OUTSIDE

If your yard is fenced, inspect it regularly for holes and gaps. The easiest way to find these openings is to attach a long line—rope or fish line—to your dog's collar and let him out into the yard. When he thinks he's free, he'll head for the opening and you'll know immediately where you need to make repairs. If your dog is a digger, you can install chicken wire in the appropriate areas under the fence so he'll hit it when he starts to dig. Through vigilance, you can keep your Basset Hound safely at home where he belongs.

We once had a Basset Hound who, if he found an opening in the fence large enough for his nose to fit through, could somehow squeeze out the rest of his body. Once he made it through, the hole became enlarged and the rest of our hounds would follow.

If your yard or garden contains any toxic plants (your local extension service can advise you) you can be sure your Basset Hound will find and taste them almost immediately. If you're not prepared to replace them with nontoxic plants, access must be blocked off before your pet arrives. Garden border fencing will not be a deterrent to a determined puppy or adult dog; a higher, more secure barricade is necessary to safeguard your pet. (See chapter 7 for further information about toxic substances.)

Make sure your Basset can't get at any toxic plants in your garden or house.

You might want to consider erecting a dog pen within your yard to ensure that your pet, when unsupervised, has no access to toxic plants or to other potential hazards. Some Basset Hounds have a propensity to eat what's not good for them, such as rocks and other foreign objects. Often, these articles will pass through the digestive system on their own with the dog suffering little more than an upset stomach. Other times, however, surgery may be required and if the problem is not detected in a timely manner, a fatal intestinal obstruction and/or infection can result.

INSIDE YOUR HOME

The interior of your home also can be a disaster waiting to happen for an inquisitive puppy. Electrical and telephone wires are irresistible to most young animals, as are such devices as television remote controls. Keep garbage out of reach at all times. A saying among dog people is: "God invented the kitchen cabinet so we can put our garbage away."

Some garbage obviously is more dangerous than other. Chicken and steak bones are hazardous to your puppy's health and well-being, and deserve special wrapping and receptacles. If your outdoor garbage container is kept in the garage or basement, the remnants of your dinner—particularly if bones are among them—should be taken there promptly. Even if your household trash is kept in a cabinet, a resourceful dog can figure out how to open the door if the odor behind it is attractive enough. For this reason, the garbage should not be kept in the same cabinet as household solvents, cleaners and chemicals. Once the puppy has finished going through the garbage, he might be tempted to try some of the other, potentially deadly items stored nearby.

Everything a puppy does is cute, but keep in mind the behavior your puppy learns now will stay with her when she matures.

Baby gates are an effective means of blocking off rooms where the puppy is not welcome. A white carpet, for instance, may not be the most ideal setting for a not-yet-housebroken puppy or a muddy puppy, and it's wiser to keep the pet out of that room rather than lose your temper when the inevitable happens. Just be sure the gate openings are not of a size that your puppy can get his head caught and possibly injure himself.

Identification

You have made sure your yard is secure and you keep your Basset on a leash when you are out, but this doesn't mean you don't need to provide some identification for your dog. Accidents happen. A visitor could leave the gate open; your dog could slip out of her collar chasing after a rabbit. If your Basset gets away, it is imperative that she have some form of identification or it is unlikely she will be recovered.

There are a few possibilities for identification. The first and most common is a simple **ID tag** attached to the collar with your dog's name and your name, address and phone number. If anyone finds your dog, this is probably the first, and perhaps the only, place he or she will look. It is a good idea to make sure your dog has a tag even if you also decide to use another method of identification as well. The drawback to a tag attached to the collar is that your dog may easily slip out of her collar in her escape, and then she is without any kind of identification.

Consider another, more permanent method. A **tattoo** can be placed on your dog's stomach close to the leg. Your dog's AKC number will be permanently tattooed on her body; she can never lose it or remove it. If someone finds your dog, you will be contacted though the AKC database. A problem with the tattoo method may occur if the person who finds your dog doesn't know what the number means or how to track you down.

The third and most sophisticated method is the **microchip.** The microchip is a tiny chip injected under the skin by your veterinarian. It contains information about your dog's identity and can never be removed. A scanner is necessary to read the chip, and though increasing numbers of animals hospitals, shelters and vet offices are becoming equipped with these, they are far from universal.

Toys and Games

When planning your puppy's entertainment, keep in mind that tug-of-war games between people and dogs are ill advised, as is too much rough play of any kind. It's a very short step between play and aggression, and rough games can lead to undesirable biting behavior. Biting and chewing should never be tolerated. No matter how cute it seems at the moment, always keep in mind that your puppy will end up a sixty-plus-pound dog, with sharp teeth and strong jaws. If you let him nip as a puppy, he has no way of knowing when to stop. Many a dog has ended up in a shelter or pound for biting family members who at one time thought this behavior was cute.

Give your Basset Hound strong, safe toys to chew on.

His own supply of toys will help a puppy pass the time of day, but use caution and common sense when selecting playthings. Basset Hound teeth are sharp and their jaws are strong, so avoid soft rubber or toys with easily removable parts that can be swallowed. A wide variety of safe toys recommended for teething puppies is available in most pet supply stores, and you can make your selection from among these. When picking toys that squeak, make sure your own ears can stand the sound!

Favorite toys also can be found right in your own home, at no cost to you whatsoever. Plastic soda or water bottles can provide entertainment by the hour for most puppies and even for adult dogs. Stuffed toys (with the button eyes and nose removed) also make good companions for puppies, particularly at sleep time. This can be especially important when you first bring your puppy home from the breeder.

Most breeders will let their puppies go at seven to eight weeks, after they've had a chance to socialize with their litter mates and learn basic discipline from their dam. Presumably, you've purchased a self-confident, outgoing puppy, but nevertheless the new surroundings of your home will be strange and you can expect some apprehension. A warm, cozy bed, a toy to cuddle with and some quiet music on the radio will help the new-comer settle in.

Puppies Need Rest

Adequate rest is absolutely essential for a young puppy. We sold a Basset Hound puppy years ago at the age of seven weeks to a potential show home. They called us after about a week to complain that she was sick. The primary symptoms were excessive urination and unsteadiness on her feet. We retrieved her immedi-ately and took her to our own veterinarian for obser-vation and diagnosis. He pronounced her fit and healthy, but exhausted. It turned out the children in the short-term home played with her constantly and did not allow her to get the rest a growing puppy needs. We kept her and were fortunate enough to watch her develop into an outstanding show dog as well as a wonderful house pet who brought us much pleasure over the years.

While you are getting to know your Basset and her idiosyn-crasies, don't hesitate to call your breeder for advice and information.

Use Your Breeder as a Resource

Had the buyers of this puppy telephoned us and described the situation, we probably would have elicited sufficient information to figure out what was going on. Instead, they called a friend who diagnosed a series of nonexistent illnesses and advised them to return the dog. Unless a medical emergency exists, it's always advisable to consult the breeder from whom you purchased your puppy about any real or imaginary health or behavioral problems. Every breed has its own idiosyncrasies, and often an experienced breeder will be more familiar with them than even the average veterinarian.

The responsible breeder has an enormous stake in every puppy produced. Although you may have paid what you consider a hefty price for your pup, don't think the breeder got rich from the litter. The money spent on maintaining a healthy brood bitch, on the stud service, on veterinary bills, food, inoculations and possibly even lost time from a paying job in order to raise the puppies can never be recouped through puppy sales.

The emotional stake in each puppy also is inestimable. When I was actively breeding, I took three weeks off from my work to stay home with the puppies. Part of that time I owned my own business and had to hire someone to come in and replace me. This may have been overkill, but Basset Hounds can be notoriously clumsy climbing into and out of the whelping box, and being there to supervise put my mind at ease.

Your breeder also may be able to refer you to a good trainer in your area by consulting a list of American Kennel Club licensed obedience clubs, many of which fulfill their public service obligation by offering to the general public low-cost training classes, including puppy kindergarten classes. For a puppy, you should not be seeking strict obedience training but merely getting your pet out to socialize with other puppies and with new people. Most kindergarten classes also include some of the rudiments of basic obedience training, such as the commands sit, down and come, but it all should be reward-propelled and, above all, it should be fun for you and your puppy.

Leash Training

Of course, before you venture off to puppy class your pet should know what a collar and leash are. In the beginning, a simple buckle collar will suffice. Probably the breeder introduced the litter to lightweight collars before you even took your puppy home. However, the breeder may not have had time to leash-train every puppy, and that will be among the chores you face.

Bring a leash and collar with you when you pick up the puppy from the breeder and be prepared to start the training lessons on day one. Basset Hounds grow and gain weight and strength quickly, so you will want to be able to put your puppy on the floor or the ground and have him under some semblance of leash control rather than straining your back by lifting and carrying this gelatin-like substance known as a Basset Hound.

Start with a lightweight, narrow leash, and gently lead the puppy in the direction you want him to go. Using treats and praise to encourage forward movement can help speed the learning process. If your puppy is determined to resist this new experience, you might just drop the leash and go about your other business, letting him trail it along behind him while he plays and explores. If you take this course, however, keep a watchful eye on the puppy because the leash could tangle, leading to panic or injury.

Lots of praise is in order when the puppy actually takes some steps forward while you're holding the leash. When he inevitably sits down and refuses to move, try coaxing and again, get out the treats. Avoid pulling and tugging on the leash. The harder you pull the more determined your Basset Hound will be to resist and stay put and, though you might win the physical war this time, your puppy could develop a strong aversion to the leash.

The most stubborn Basset Hound ultimately will give in and do your bidding, but only if you are equally stubborn and refuse to let him have his way.

Now that your puppy has learned to walk on a leash, there is little reason to carry him. If he must be carried, it should be by an adult, never by a child. The Basset Hound spinal column is prone to injury, and failure to support the back properly when lifting and carrying a Basset Hound can result in severe trauma. Your breeder probably showed you the correct way to lift and carry your pet, but the most important point to remember is always to give the spinal column sufficient support.

Following these basic tips should get you off to a good start and provide you with the foundation you need to establish a long-term, loving relationship between family and pet, one that will lead you to proclaim proudly, "I am owned by a Basset Hound!"

Boarding Your Basset Hound

As a new dog owner, you will steadily become familiar with every aspect of living with your dog—even leaving your dog behind. What do you do with your Basset when he can't travel with you? Though you may want to take your Basset with you everywhere you go, there are often times when it is inconvenient or impossible for him to come along. It is unfair to leave your dog alone for long periods in an unfamiliar environment while you sightsee or visit with relatives. For trips like these, make sure you plan ahead to provide the best care for your Basset when you can't be there.

KENNEL

This is the most common way of providing care for pets when owners are away. To choose a good kennel, get recommendations from other pet owners in your area or your veterinarian, then go check out the facilities yourself. Look for clean facilities with both an indoor and outdoor run for the dogs, and professional and genuinely attentive personnel. Choose a kennel that requires proof of shots, including a kennel cough preventive.

Note: Do keep in mind that even if the kennel requires a kennel cough preventive, there is no guarantee that your pet won't get sick. Kennel cough is much like the flu in humans; there are so many strains of the diseases that it is impossible to vaccinate against all of them. The preventive protects against a common strain, and is often effective, but it is always a possibility that your dog will contract a contagious condition (including fleas!) when you board him in a kennel.

After you have chosen the best kennel, prepare your Basset for his stay by packing up some favorite toys, blankets and treats. If possible, see if you can get a friend or family member to visit him once or twice a week while you are away. Always leave your vet's telephone number and a number at which you can be reached with the kennel staff when you drop off your dog.

IN-HOME PET CARE

The advantages to in-home pet care are that your dog will be able to remain in a familiar home environment, and he will not be exposed to germs or fleas from other dogs. But there are some drawbacks to this method as well. Do you mind having a stranger in your home while you are away? Normally well-behaved dogs left alone for long periods often become depressed and destructive, and Bassets have a tendency to howl when left alone for extended periods of time. Not only is your dog expressly unhappy, but can your neighbors handle it? Can the pet care service provide someone who will spend some time with your dog, in addition to walking and feeding him?

As you would with a kennel, get a recommendation for in-home care personnel from your vet or fellow dog owners. Set up an interview first, and make sure you choose someone you trust.

chapter 5

Feeding
Your
Basset Hound

A roly-poly Basset Hound puppy may be cute, but he's also a health disaster waiting to happen. The bone structure of the Basset Hound cannot carry too much weight without permanent damage. An obese adult Basset Hound risks heart disease, back problems and a myriad of other health problems common to overweight dogs. Extra weight on the young Basset Hound will stress the short leg bones and possibly cause permanent limb problems.

First Food

When you pick up your puppy from the breeder, you should receive instructions on the feeding schedule and the brand and amount of food to feed. A good-quality dry kibble puppy formula is best, and it's advisable to stay with the food the breeder has been using. If you decide to change to another top-quality brand, make the transition slowly, adding just a small amount of the new food very gradually.

Young puppies must eat more frequently than adult dogs. Again, your breeder will advise you of the feeding schedule and whether your puppy is still on four meals a day or has been cut back to three. Three meals daily are advisable until at least four months of age, although we usually continue the three-a-day schedule until eight or nine months. Eventually, the number of meals will be reduced to two a day.

Your Basset Hound probably will let you know when it's time to switch to adult food. Some puppies by the age of seven or eight months will start to turn up their noses at the puppy kibble and they're ready to advance to adult formula, which contains a lower percentage of protein than the growth kibble.

Nutritional Needs

Dog food manufacturers spend millions of dollars testing and determining optimum levels of nutrients for dogs in different life phases. Theoretically, you can provide your dog with the same nutrition he gets from commercial dog food, but it's unlikely you will have quite the body of knowledge, research and trial and error behind you that leading companies do. Unless your dog is ill or recuperating, and is off his usual food, it's easiest for you and healthiest for your dog to stick with commercial food.

TYPES OF FOODS/TREATS

There are three types of commercially available dog food—dry, canned and semimoist—and a huge assortment of treats (lucky dogs!) to feed your dog. Which should you choose?

Dry and canned foods contain similar ingredients. The primary difference between them is their moisture content. The moisture is not just water. It's blood and broth, too, the very things that dogs adore. So while canned food is more palatable, dry food is more economical, convenient and effective in controlling tartar buildup. Most owners feed a 25% canned/75% dry diet to give their dogs the benefit of both. Just be sure your dog is getting the nutrition he needs (you and your veterinarian can determine this).

Semimoist foods have the flavor dogs love and the convenience owners want. However, they tend to contain excessive amounts of artificial colors and preservatives.

Dog treats come in every size, shape and flavor imaginable, from organic cookies shaped like postmen to beefy chew sticks. Dogs seem to love them all, so enjoy the variety. Just be sure not to overindulge your dog. Factor treats into her regular meal sizes.

Your Basset needs protein, carbohydrates, fats, vitamins and minerals in the right proportions to remain healthy and fit. If, as suggested, you are feeding the right portion of a high-quality kibble, all these things should be present in the correct amounts. Make sure you use the formula that is appropriate for your dog's age and activity level.

Protein is necessary for building and repairing body tissue. Growing puppies, active dogs and pregnant and lactating females need extra. Protein is not stored in the body, so it needs to be replenished every day. Nonworking adult dogs need about 15 percent protein in their diet.

Fats are used for storing energy and also contribute to a shiny coat and healthy skin. Too much fat stored under the skin will make your Basset obese, so monitor fat content carefully.

Carbohydrates provide energy. Sources of carbohydrates include potatoes, pasta, rice and other grains.

Vitamins are necessary to aid and regulate bodily functions, including growth and immunity. Vitamin deficiencies can result in a lackluster coat, weight loss, unhealthy skin and vision problems. If you are feeding a high-quality kibble, it probably includes all the vitamins necessary for your dog's health.

Minerals are also necessary to keep your Basset's body functioning correctly and efficiently. A high-quality dry food should contain all necessary minerals in the correct proportions.

HOW MANY MEALS A DAY?

Individual dogs vary in how much they should eat to maintain a desired body weight—not too fat, but not too thin. Puppies need several meals a day, while older dogs may need only one. Determine how much food keeps your adult dog looking and feeling her best. Then decide how many meals you want to feed with that amount. Like us, most dogs love to eat, and offering two meals a day is more enjoyable for them. If you're worried about overfeeding, make sure you measure correctly and abstain from adding tidbits to the meals.

Whether you feed one or two meals, only leave your dog's food out for the amount of time it takes her to eat it—10 minutes, for example. Freefeeding (when food is available any time) and leisurely meals encourage picky eating. Don't worry if your dog doesn't finish all her dinner in the allotted time. She'll learn she should.

Is Supplementation Necessary?

More of a good thing is not necessarily better! Too many vitamins and minerals, just like too few, can result in dangerous conditions. If your veterinarian prescribes a certain supplement for a specific condition, follow his or her advice. If you think your puppy would benefit from supplementation, discuss this with your veterinarian.

Vitamin C

Many experts and experienced breeders claim that Vitamin C can have miraculous effects. When administered to puppies, many say it can help prevent the development of conditions such as hip displasia. Vitamin C is water soluble, and cannot hurt your puppy. If he has too much in his system, it will be passed through the body rather than stored, though too much will give your puppy loose stools. Though many people claim Vitamin C works wonders, this has yet to be proven. Before beginning any supplementation, discuss it with your veterinarian.

Reading Labels

To find out what's in your dog's food, read the labels just as you would on your own food. Ingredients are listed in descending order by weight. Be wary if ingredients like "by-products" are included near the top of the list. This is a cheap way for dog food manufacturers to fulfill protein requirements. Many of the components of "by-products," like feather, feet or hair, do not actually contain digestible protein are therefore nutritionally useless to your dog.

What to Feed Your Basset

When you check out the dog food section at your supermarket or pet store, you will probably be overwhelmed. There are so many different brands, formulas, flavors, and types of food that it's hard to know where to begin. Use the following information and the recommendations of your breeder and vet to choose foods that will keep your Basset in peak condition throughout his life.

DRY FOOD (KIBBLE)

Nutritionally complete dry food should be the staple of your dog's diet. Chose a high-quality brand, and select the formula that is appropriate for your dog's age and activity level. Less expensive brands sometimes substi-

tute with substandard ingredients that are not useful for your dog. Crunching on dry food will also help keep your Basset's teeth clean; as he chomps, the rough edges will scrape along his teeth helping to keep them free of tartar.

CANNED FOOD

Canned food is much more expensive than dry food, and many kinds contain up to 70 percent water. Many kinds of canned food are not nutritionally complete

Many Basset Hound owners wet their dog's food and let it soak for twenty minutes before feeding to help prevent torsion.

and are meant to be served with dry food, so again, make sure you read the label. If it does not say "complete" or "nutritionally complete" it is meant to complement dry food. Because canned food is soft and moist, it does not help keep your dog's teeth and gums in good condition. A popular way to get the benefits of kibble and the added palatability of canned food is to serve one third canned food with two thirds dry food. Remember to refrigerate canned food once it has been opened.

SEMIMOIST FOOD

Semimoist food is often colored and packaged to look like hamburgers. This means nothing to the dog, and is designed to attract the owner (who is doing the purchasing). Semimoist foods tend to have large amounts of sugar, salt, artificial colorings and preservatives. If your choose to feed this kind of food to your dog, consider offering small bits as a treat rather

feeding large quantities as a meal. Another ploy designed to attract the owner is that semimoist food often comes packaged in individual servings. While this can be very useful (while traveling, for example) try packaging single portions of your Basset's usual kibble in sealing sandwich bags instead.

WATER

Always, always have fresh water available for your dog. Check the water bowl at least twice a day to make sure he has a good sup-

ply. Change the water and thoroughly rinse the bowl daily. If your dog will be outside for any extended period, make sure he also has access to clean water there.

Treats are an important part of training and companionship.

SNACKS AND TREATS

Dry dog biscuits are useful as treats between meals or during training sessions. Like kibble, hard biscuits are good for your dog's teeth and will help control tartar.

Other healthy treats you can feed your dog include bits of fruit or steamed vegetables, like grapes, apples, carrots and broccoli. Basset Hounds can be prone to obesity, so keep treats to a minimum. When you are reckoning your dog's daily caloric intake, don't forget to include treats as well. Offer little tidbits—a small piece of biscuit instead of the whole thing. The most important thing to your dog is that you are praising him and offering a reward.

Digestive Problems

Although many breeds do well on one feeding daily, the Basset Hound is among the breeds at risk for torsion, an often fatal, always dangerous digestive problem that occurs primarily in deep-chested dogs. The stomach fills with gas—a condition known as bloat—and if not detected and dealt with immediately the stomach will actually twist. For a dog in the early bloat stage, gas can usually be relieved by having the stomach pumped out or through an incision in the side. However, once the stomach twists, surgery is the only option if the dog's life is to be saved.

> ### TO SUPPLEMENT OR NOT TO SUPPLEMENT?
>
> If you're feeding your dog a diet that's correct for her developmental stage and she's alert, healthy-looking and neither over- nor underweight, you don't need to add supplements. These include table scraps as well as vitamins and minerals. In fact, a growing puppy is in danger of developing musculoskeletal disorders by oversupplementation. If you have any concerns about the nutritional quality of the food you're feeding, discuss them with your veterinarian.

The Morris Animal Foundation, which has done extensive research into torsion, advises owners of at-risk breeds to feed two or more small meals a day rather than one large one as one way to minimize the possibility of the dog's falling victim to this dreaded ailment. Exercise before and after meals should be curtailed as well. Our own dogs typically are fed in their crates and forced to have quiet time before and after their twice-a-day feedings.

On the other hand, we once had a dog who, while staying at a boarding kennel, got out of his run and ate his way through the facility, consuming several pounds of kibble and an unknown quantity of biscuits. The veterinarian who was consulted advised giving him peroxide to induce vomiting and get his stomach emptied out immediately, before he had a chance to bloat. This was done, to no avail. The dog not only failed to "empty out," he digested what he had eaten, seemed to enjoy the peroxide as an after-dinner drink and kept that down as well. This dog, though not a Basset Hound but also a breed at risk for torsion, was fortunate enough to have a stomach made of iron.

Although kibble can be fed either dry or wet, most Basset Hound owners opt to wet their dogs' food with warm water and let it soak for at least twenty minutes before feeding. This allows the food to swell outside the stomach rather than in it. Our adult dogs eat between four and five cups of kibble daily, divided into two meals. The amount of food your Basset Hound needs will depend on his size and activity level. Puppies require more food than most adults because of the additional demands of growth and high activity level.

Just as in housetraining, a regular feeding schedule is important to a dog and should be adhered to as closely as possible. At the same time, don't make yourself crazy trying to follow the breeder's feeding schedule if it does not mesh with your own lifestyle. Dogs are adaptable and you can make changes in the routine; just try to keep them to a minimum and once you get a new one established, stay with it as closely as you can.

Weight Problems

If your dog gets too heavy (or too thin), your veterinarian will be able to advise you to adjust the amount being fed. If in doubt, a visit to your breeder may be in order. Having the dog's well-being at heart, the breeder probably will throw tact aside and let you know exactly how your dog looks. Don't take the criticism personally; accept it as being in your pet's best interest and try to make the recommended adjustments.

For the dog who is getting too heavy, most of the quality pet food manufacturers include a low-calorie or "light" food in their line. You can switch to this, usually without upsetting your dog's stomach. Once it's determined that your pet needs to be on a diet, treats must be curtailed as well, but this can be done so surreptitiously that your dog will never even become suspicious. Under normal weight conditions, a limited number of biscuits or other treats is acceptable, particularly to reward good behavior. The dieting dog need not be deprived. Instead of going through a box of biscuits a day for the extremely well-behaved dog, try small pieces of raw carrot or apple, switch to low-calorie biscuits and break them into small pieces or just give a couple of kernels of the dog's regular diet kibble as a treat. *What* you give matters little to the dog. What's important to him is the mere fact that you're giving him something extra.

What if Your Basset's Not Eating?

Although most Basset Hounds are not finicky eaters, some do learn that by turning up their noses at their dog food, concerned owners will break out the treats or table scraps in order to keep them from starving. Although it's difficult to watch your dog walk away from a full dish, keep in mind that a healthy dog will not starve himself to death. Give him a half hour to eat and then pick up the dish. Repeat the routine at the next mealtime and keep repeating it until your dog gets the message and settles for his dog food. Once you succumb and add the table scraps he's yearning for, you'll be hooked for life.

If you honestly feel you must entice your dog to eat, try mixing in with the kibble some grated cheese,

---

HOW TO READ THE DOG FOOD LABEL

With so many choices on the market, how can you be sure you are feeding the right food for your dog? The information is all there on the label—if you know what you're looking for.

Look for the nutritional claim right up top. Is the food "100% nutritionally complete"? If so, it's for nearly all life stages; "growth and maintenance," on the other hand, is for early development; puppy foods are marked as such, as are foods for senior dogs.

Ingredients are listed in descending order by weight. The first three or four ingredients will tell you the bulk of what the food contains. Look for the highest-quality ingredients, like meats and grains, to be among them.

The Guaranteed Analysis tells you what levels of protein, fat, fiber and moisture are in the food, in that order. While these numbers are meaningful, they won't tell you much about the quality of the food. Nutritional value is in the dry matter, not the moisture content.

In many ways, seeing is believing. If your dog has bright eyes, a shiny coat, a good appetite and a good energy level, chances are his diet's fine. Your dog's breeder and your veterinarian are good sources of advice if you're still confused.

garlic salt or even a spoonful of canned cat food. At the same time, you should know your dog's attitude and appearance well enough to distinguish between a finicky eater who's trying to hold out for people food and a sick pet. If your dog acts sluggish, has runny eyes, feels warm to the touch or seems abnormal in any way, it may be time for a visit to the veterinarian. On the other hand, if the attitude and appearance are perfectly normal, wait him out. Chances are he'll return to eating his dog food once he's convinced that nothing else is coming his way.

Taboos

By purchasing a well-balanced dog food you are guaranteeing your puppy the nourishment he needs to grow into a strong, healthy adult. Table scraps will only serve to throw off the nutritional balance of the food, and will encourage your puppy to develop bad habits. Unless you want sad eyes gazing up at you and a wet mouth on your knee every time the family sits down to a meal, limit your pet to his own food in his own dish at his own mealtime.

Some treats are definitely taboo for dogs. Heading this list is chocolate, which often has a toxic effect on dogs and should be avoided at all times. Holidays are particularly dangerous, especially Easter, Valentine's Day and Halloween, when candy commonly finds its way into households. Children should be warned and watched carefully to make sure they don't leave their chocolate Easter bunnies within reach, and adults should set a good example by keeping *all* people treats off-limits to pets. If your dog should ingest chocolate, an immediate call to the veterinarian is recommended so you know what precautions to take and what poisoning symptoms to look for. You also want to alert the doctor to the potential problem just in case you need to make an emergency visit. (One unwritten rule is that these things happen after regular office hours.)

Above all, remember that your dog is just that—a *dog*. He will not get bored as people do with the same meal over and over again. You do not need to cook for him (except perhaps when he is ill), and you certainly should not have a variety of dog foods taking up your pantry space. Stick with the one basic, tried-and-true, top-quality dry dog food, and you'll be repaid many times over with a well-conditioned, healthy animal.

Grooming
Your
Basset Hound

Basset Hounds are basic "wash-and-wear" dogs, and require only a minimum amount of serious grooming. However, unless they are given some maintenance, they soon can become an unattractive, unhealthy source of offensive odor and dirt.

Grooming Supplies

The grooming supplies you will need are minimal,

thanks to the Basset Hound's short coat. Among the essentials are a rubber currycomb or a hound glove, a steel coat "rake," nail clippers, a teeth-cleaning tool, ear cleaner, lots of cotton swabs and shampoo.

Frequent baths will not be necessary if you use the currycomb or hound glove on a regular basis to remove accumulated dirt as well as dead skin and shedding coat. The rake will pull out the dead coat from the thick areas, such as the neck. Twice-a-week cleanings with these tools will considerably reduce the number of baths required to keep your Basset Hound clean.

Regular use of a currycomb will remove dead hair and minimize bathing requirements.

Bath Time

Most Bassets, however, will need an occasional bath given their propensity for going through almost every convenient mud puddle. The underside of the low-slung body attracts dirt like a magnet as the Basset Hound splashes through rain puddles or slush. I was always amused at dog shows watching my fellow exhibitors carrying sixty-five-pound hounds over their shoulders to the ring during inclement weather, only to plop them down into the inevitable mud once they arrived there. By the time the judge examined the dogs, their hounds were no cleaner than mine, who had waded through the water to reach the ring.

When it's bath time, put on your oldest clothes and/or a waterproof grooming apron, and get out lots of towels. Garage sales are a wonderful source of "dog towels," so you don't have to use your own good linens on your dog. Be generous in throwing towels on the bathroom floor as well as in the crate where the dog will be put to dry. When these preparations are completed, it's time to get the dog into the bathtub. If you're doing the job without help, place the dog's front feet on the edge of the tub and gently boost the rest of him in while supporting his front with one hand on his chest. If you have assistance available, one person can pick up the front end while the other lifts the rear to place the dog gently in the tub.

A spray nozzle attached to the faucet makes it easy to wet the dog down thoroughly. If you don't have a spray at your disposal, use a large paper cup or plastic container to wet the dog with warm water. Avoid using a glass container because when the dog suddenly shakes himself he could knock it out of your hand, and the broken glass will go everywhere. A plastic hook or ring attached to the wall over the tub at the appropriate height will give you an anchor for a grooming noose (available from most pet supply stores), enabling you to hold the dog somewhat steady and under control during the bath.

Purchase a good-quality shampoo. My favorite is a citrus shampoo because it will kill fleas without exposing the dog to potentially harmful chemicals, and yet it smells good and does an effective cleansing job. You might want to keep a second shampoo on hand, one designed to bring out your dog's color highlights. If your Basset Hound's coat has a lot of white, you will want to use a whitener, particularly under the chin and on the feet. For those dogs with skin problems, your veterinarian can recommend a good medicated shampoo. What supplies you need will be dictated by your own particular dog.

For a puppy, make sure the shampoo is mild enough not to damage his skin or coat. Read the label carefully, follow the directions and heed any hazard warnings they contain.

Two soapings followed by thorough rinsing will clean the average dog. There are a number of rinses, conditioners and other coat products on the market, but seldom does the Basset Hound benefit from these extras. What he might need, however, is a nonchemical

GROOMING TOOLS

pin brush

slicker brush

flea comb

towel

mat rake

grooming glove

scissors

nail clippers

tooth-cleaning equipment

shampoo

conditioner

clippers

"odor-eater" in the rinse water to eliminate the hound smell.

While your dog is in the tub be sure and clean the ears and check for any ticks that may have attached themselves to him. Favorite hiding spots are in and around the ears and between the toes.

After toweling your dog off as much as possible, you have several options, depending on the weather and the extent of the equipment available to you. On a warm, sunny day, you can take your dog outside to run around and dry off. Make sure there are no convenient mud puddles or you'll be starting the whole process over again. In inclement weather, your dog should be kept indoors until dry. You can encourage the drying process by using a hairdryer if you don't own a regular heavy-duty dog dryer. Or, lacking even that, spread towels in the crate and bed your dog down until he's dry.

A good bath will loosen up the coat that's ready to fall out, so if you ignore the next step in the grooming process you're asking for a house full of dog hair. Once the dog is thoroughly dry, it's time to get out the curry comb or hound glove and get rid of the dead coat and dead skin. This also is the appropriate time to take care of nails and general foot hygiene.

A Basset conditioned to nail trimming from puppyhood should accept the procedure calmly.

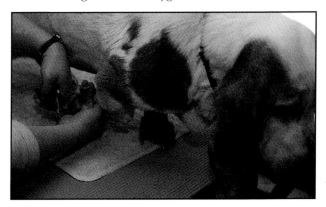

Nail Trimming

Of course, you've conditioned your dog from puppyhood to having his feet handled and his nails cut without a fuss. Dogs who hate having their nails cut or their feet touched usually can trace their phobia back to something the owner did wrong. Gentle handling of a puppy's feet and matter-of-fact nail tipping on a regular basis should result in a well-mannered dog who accepts this kind of attention without fuss. On the other hand, if nail cutting is accompanied by lots of sympathy from you, the puppy will grow up believing this is a horrible experience, and it will be—for both of you.

When cutting the nails, start with the back feet and you'll be halfway through before your dog even knows what you're doing. In addition to cutting the nails, check the pads of the feet to make sure they're not harboring any foreign objects, ticks or sores. Foot hygiene will be enhanced if you clean excess hair from the pads, carefully using blunt-nosed scissors or an electric shaver.

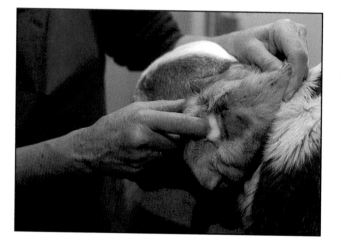

*Basset Hounds'
long ears
require frequent
cleaning to keep
them free of
infection.*

Ear Cleanings

Frequent ear cleanings (at least once a week) with a cotton ball and warm water or cleaning solution provided by your veterinarian will help ward off painful, pesky and potentially costly ear infections. A sure sign that you've missed the boat is frequent head-shaking by your Basset Hound. Once this starts, a visit to the veterinarian is probably inevitable, unless the doctor previously provided you with a good all-purpose antibiotic ointment to keep on hand for such emergencies.

Teeth Cleaning

Maintaining your dog's teeth will help minimize the risk of bad breath, gum disease and the other problems inherent to bad teeth. Your veterinarian can instruct you in brushing your pet's teeth and maintaining a healthy mouth. Not only will this keep your dog in top-notch shape; it ultimately will save you money on expensive veterinary bills for dental work.

Teeth cleaning is necessary for health, hygiene and canine good looks.

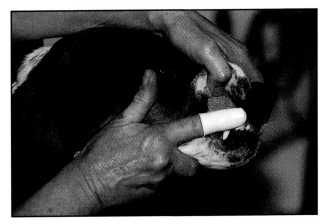

Skin Check

Grooming time is also an opportunity to check your pet for hot spots and other skin problems. Basset Hounds are most prone to hot spots in areas where moisture tends to accumulate, such as under the chin, on the feet and in other areas where skin folds exist. An antiseptic powder, available from your veterinarian, usually will dry these up and promote healing. If allowed to go untreated for any length of time, the skin can become inflamed and infected and more radical measures will be needed to effect a total cure.

If all of this sounds too time-consuming, be thankful you didn't select a coated breed requiring trimming and sculpting. Most of what your Basset Hound needs to look and feel his best falls into the category of maintenance rather than beauty treatment. If you establish and follow a regular grooming routine, the end result will be a beautiful, healthy pet.

Grooming Trends

For the show ring, many Basset Hound exhibitors will remove the dog's whiskers to give the muzzle a clean, neat appearance. In recent years, however, a number of people have abandoned this practice in favor of a more "natural" dog, using the reasoning that the Basset Hound's whiskers serve a sensory function in the field, helping him feel where he is. Dogs also appear in the show ring with some evidence of trimming on the rear end, the underside of the tail and along the "skirt" underneath. None of this is required grooming for the ring, and certainly not for a house pet.

Basset Hounds need minimal grooming to look naturally great in or out of the show ring.

chapter 7

Keeping Your
Basset Hound
Healthy

Good grooming and diet regimens are essential for keeping your Basset in the best of health. Good preventive health care at home and regular visits to the veterinarian will further ensure your beloved Basset's good health.

You Know Your Basset Best

As you get you get to know your puppy, you'll become familiar with how he acts and feels when he's healthy. While you are brushing and combing your Basset, run your hands over your dog and feel for any lumps, irregularities or abrasions. Look for ticks your dog might have picked up outside, for flea dirt and (if you're quick enough!) fleas. (See the section on "External Parasites" later in the chapter for information on how to deal with these pests.)

Be alert for any changes in appearance or behavior. If your dog tires more quickly than usual, for example, or doesn't seem to be eating the way he normally does, it could be a signal that something is wrong. It is up to you, the owner, to determine if and when your Basset seems under the weather and alert your vet. You are the person who knows your Basset best, so be attentive to your pet and let your vet know if something's wrong.

Choosing a Veterinarian

Identify a competent veterinarian before you even introduce your puppy to her new home. This may involve some research on your part and personal interviews with more than one veterinarian in your area.

If you've had no previous relationship with a local veterinarian, consult your breeder for referrals to other owners in your area who might be able to recommend a veterinarian with Basset Hound experience. Is the Basset Hound so unique that it needs a specialist? Not really, but it does help to have a doctor

Take your puppy to the vet within a few days of bringing her home.

who is aware of the problems that typically show up in your breed and also understands the Basset's physical idiosyncrasies. You also do not want a vet who is biased against Basset Hounds. We have run into veterinarians who openly dislike particular breeds, and if the Basset Hound is on that list, we steer clear of them.

During the interview process, you will want to know what emergency arrangements are available. Does the hospital you're considering provide twenty-four-hour service, or does it use an emergency clinic for after-hours coverage? If the latter is the case, is the emergency clinic convenient for you? Twenty minutes is my limit for getting to a veterinary hospital, whether it be my regular doctor or an emergency facility.

If the hospital has more than one doctor, can you see the veterinarian of your choice or will you be assigned by the office staff? Are the hours convenient to your own schedule? All of these questions need to be answered to your satisfaction.

At the same time, make sure you feel comfortable with the veterinarian's bedside manner. Don't expect less for your pet than you would ask for yourself. In addition to being considerate of your dog and his comfort, the doctor should be willing to share information with you, the owner and bill payer. Before you commit to a doctor, make sure that he or she is willing to provide complete, nontechnical explanations of all diagnoses and procedures.

Going to the vet need not be a fearful experience for an animal, despite the occasional discomfort of inoculations and tests. The attitude of the veterinarian and the assisting staff will determine whether your dog comes in for his regular visits with tail wagging or tail tucked.

Your Puppy's First Visit

Once you've decided on a veterinarian and set the date to bring your puppy home, it's time to schedule an initial appointment. Most breeders require that you have your new puppy examined within a few days. This period usually is fairly short (perhaps seventy-two hours), so that there is no time for the puppy to contract a disease or injury through *your* negligence for which the breeder will be held responsible. Make sure you read, understand and abide by the contract for the protection of everyone involved.

When you take the puppy for her first visit, the veterinarian probably will request that you bring a stool sample so that a worm check can be done. Worms in young puppies are common and are no cause for alarm. Also bring with you the inoculation and worming records given to you by the breeder so your veterinarian can establish a comprehensive hospital record and set up a schedule to complete the necessary vaccinations.

Your Puppy's Shots

Puppies receive their earliest immunizations from their mother's first milk (colostrum), but thereafter will need a series of three or four vaccinations to maintain immunization against distemper, hepatitis, parainfluenza and parvovirus. In some areas, a leptospirosis vaccine is included. The inoculations should be spaced three to four weeks apart, and it is important to complete the series, because the immunization passed on to the puppies by their mother may override the early inoculations. If the immunization schedule is not maintained, the puppy will be left with no protection against these serious diseases.

Most veterinarians administer "galaxy" inoculations, giving the various vaccines at one time. Don't be alarmed if your puppy exhibits signs of grogginess afterwards, or experiences swelling in the area of the shot.

> ### YOUR PUPPY'S VACCINES
>
> Vaccines are given to prevent your dog from getting an infectious disease like canine distemper or rabies. Vaccines are the ultimate preventive medicine: they're given before your dog ever gets the disease so as to protect him from the disease. That's why it is necessary for your dog to be vaccinated routinely. Puppy vaccines start at eight weeks of age for the five-in-one DHLPP vaccine and are given every three to four weeks until the puppy is sixteen months old. Your veterinarian will put your puppy on a proper schedule and will remind you when to bring in your dog for shots.

The DHPP (or DHLPP) inoculation requires an annual booster if your pet is to remain immune. Most veterinarians mail out reminders to their clients when inoculations are due, but it's a good idea to mark the date on your own calendar just to be safe.

Rabies inoculations, once given typically at six months of age, now are administered at three to four months. The first rabies shot is valid for one year; thereafter, if given promptly, rabies inoculations are good for two or three years, depending on your state of residence and your own veterinarian's preference and recommendation.

Certain other inoculations are optional and should be discussed with your veterinarian. Lyme vaccine, given in an initial series of two inoculations, is available, as is coronavirus vaccine. If your puppy (or adult dog) is to be kenneled at any time during the year you should immunize him against bordatella (kennel cough). An intranasal vaccine usually is administered annually to ward off this upper respiratory ailment.

WHAT ARE ALL THOSE VACCINATIONS FOR?

DISTEMPER

This highly contagious viral disease used to kill thousands of dogs. Thankfully, today's vaccines are extremely effective. Early symptoms of distemper include weakness, coughing, fever and watery discharge from eyes and nose. As the disease progresses, the discharge turns thicker and yellowish—a sign that the dog is infected with distemper rather than kennel cough. In some strains of the disease, tough calluses form on the infected dog's nose and soles of the feet, hence the common name "hard-pad" for this disease. Though some dogs can survive a distemper infection, it is almost always fatal in young puppies, who are particularly susceptible.

CANINE HEPATITIS

This dangerous viral disease attacks primarily the liver, and also the kidneys and blood vessels. It is not related to the form of hepatitis that affects people. Initial symptoms include lethargy, fever, vomiting and jaundice. Again, the disease is most commonly found in unvaccinated young puppies.

LEPTOSPIROSIS

This highly contagious bacterial disease is transferred through the urine of infected wildlife. Many other animals, including humans, are susceptible. Your Basset could be exposed to the bacteria if he sniffs at a bush marked with the urine of an infected animal, or drinks from a contaminated stream. The bacteria attacks the kidneys, resulting in kidney failure. Early symptoms include fever, lethargy and appetite loss. As the disease begins to damage the kidneys, the dog may bleed from the mouth, pass bloody stools and become excessively thirsty.

PARVOVIRUS

Puppies are particularly susceptible to "Parvo," which has caused thousands of canine fatalities in the past decade. Fortunately, an effective vaccine has been developed. This virus attacks the intestine, causing bloody diarrhea with a distinct odor. The virus moves through the dog's system very quickly, often causing dehydration, shock and death in a matter of hours.

CORONAVIRUS

As with many contagious diseases, this virus is particularly dangerous to young puppies and adult dogs in stressful conditions. Symptoms include appetite loss, vomiting and yellowish, watery stools that may contain mucus or blood. Dehydration and death can follow.

LYME DISEASE

In some areas of the country, a vaccination for Lyme disease is recommended along with the usual series of puppy inoculations. This disease is transmitted through tiny ticks (deer ticks) carried primarily by deer and mice, and typically occurs during the summer months when ticks are prevalent. Symptoms of Lyme disease include lameness and swollen, painful joints, fever and weakness.

KENNEL COUGH

Kennel cough is not a fatal illness, but can weaken your Basset and make him susceptible to other conditions. It is especially hard on older dogs and puppies. You might also find yourself up all night as he coughs endlessly. Vaccines are available for many common strains of kennel cough but, like the flu in humans, there are too many strains of this disease to make a vaccine effective against all of them. Vaccinating your dog is the best preventive you can offer, though it is no guarantee. If your Basset does succumb, your vet will most likely prescribe antibiotics, and ask you to keep him warm and comfortable.

RABIES

Rabies is probably the most commonly known of all these diseases, in part because of the threat it poses to humans. Any warm-blooded animal can be infected. The virus is transmitted through the saliva, often through a bite, and then travels through the nervous system. As it reaches the brain, behavioral changes ensue. Wild animals may become aggressive or friendly and wander into populated areas they would normally avoid. Beware of a wild animal who seems "tame." This is unnatural behavior that indicates a problem of some kind. Affectionate pets may turn snappy and aggressive. As the disease progresses, the animal will have trouble swallowing and will start salivating and drooling excessively. Death follows closely behind. There is no treatment for rabies once symptoms appear, so it is imperative that your Basset be vaccinated and that necessary boosters be kept up to date.

External Parasites

FLEAS

No matter how careful you are, your dog may become a host for fleas. Your first indication that fleas are present will be almost constant scratching. That's your

The flea is a die-hard pest.

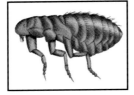

signal to spring into action and begin a heavy-duty cleanup of dog and environment, both indoors and out. This is an ideal time to get your pet(s) to the groomer for a good flea bath. While they're out of the house, exterminate your home and surrounding area to rid the environment of fleas. It's best to avoid chemicals that are toxic to you and your animals. Safer products are available, including an easy-to-use methoprene spray that prevents larvae and pupae from developing into adult fleas and renders them incapable of reproducing. Outdoor sprays containing biopesticides are also harmless to the environment and effective in ridding the area of fleas.

Flea collars are a quick fix but are largely ineffective and frequently result in an allergic reaction, particularly among Basset Hounds. While the fleas scurry to the other end of the dog and comfortably set up housekeeping at the tail end, the chronically damp chin and neck of the Basset Hound do not mix well with the chemicals in the collar, and redness, irritation and hair loss in the throat area often results. The chemicals contained in flea collars can be extremely toxic if ingested by a dog.

Such popular flea fighters as garlic and brewer's yeast have no effect on larvae or eggs, although they might decrease the population on the dog.

A monthly pill, available from veterinarians, is designed to stop the reproductive cycle of the fleas, but this needs to be combined with a clean environment to be effective. Your dog's bedding should be washed in hot water, and carpets and furniture should be vacuumed regularly and thoroughly to remove not only the larvae but the feces of adult fleas, which are a source of nourishment for fleas. Shampoos and sprays containing pyrethrin may be used on the dog (in moderation, please), but citrus shampoos also are effective in killing fleas, although they have no residual effect.

Fleas should not be shrugged off as an inevitable partner of dog ownership, particularly if your Basset

---

FIGHTING FLEAS

Remember, the fleas you see on your dog are only part of the problem—the smallest part! To rid your dog and home of fleas, you need to treat your dog *and* your home. Here's how:

• Identify where your pet(s) sleep. These are "hot spots."

• Clean your pets' bedding regularly by vacuuming and washing.

• Spray "hot spots" with a non-toxic, long-lasting flea larvicide.

• Treat outdoor "hot spots" with insecticide.

• Kill eggs on pets with a product containing insect growth regulators (IGRs).

• Kill fleas on pets per your veterinarian's recommendation.

Hound has an allergic reaction to them as many dogs do. Fleas not only are dirty and itchy, but they also are the hosts for tapeworm in dogs.

TICKS

Ticks, too, present serious health problems because of their ability to transmit diseases. Examine your dog regularly during the tick infestation months, probing

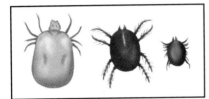

between the toes, in the ears, under the armpits and around the head and neck areas.

Although **Lyme disease** is perhaps the best known of tick-borne diseases, other ailments carried by these ugly insects include Rocky Mountain spotted fever and several forms of ehrlichiosis, the latter showing up particularly in the South, where the brown dog tick can survive almost year-round.

Three types of ticks (l-r): the wood tick, brown dog tick and deer tick.

Lyme disease, first identified in Lyme, Connecticut, is difficult to diagnose and can exhibit a variety of symptoms, not just the classic signs of lameness. However, once the disease is diagnosed it can be treated successfully with antibiotics. A vaccine is also available if you live in an area where Lyme disease is common.

Tick collars are available that are safe for dogs and are effective in repelling ticks. For maximum results, it should remain on the dog at all times except during baths.

To remove ticks from your dog's body, it is advisable first to kill the tick by applying some form of alcohol or insecticide using a cotton-tipped applicator. Then, use tweezers to grab the tick as close to the skin as possible. Don't worry if the head remains imbedded; it will drop out by itself. Be careful to avoid contact with the blood from ticks, which can transmit diseases to humans as well as to dogs.

Use tweezers to remove ticks from your dog.

MITES

Ear mites are the most frequent cause of ear infections in puppies and adolescent dogs. Frequent head shaking and scratching of both ears is indicative of the presence of mites, which can be seen under a microscope. No larger than the heads of pins, ear mites are white and move rapidly. They are highly contagious not only to other dogs but to cats as well. Treatment consists of a three-week round of miticide, often combined with an antibiotic to combat accompanying infection. Steroids also may be used to treat the itching.

Another form of mite causes **sarcoptic mange,** when the female digs her way under the dog's skin to lay her eggs. After the eggs hatch—in three to ten days—the newborn mites repeat the process, usually lodging in the areas of the ears, elbows, hocks and face of the dog. The result is extreme discomfort, characterized by hair loss, a rash and oozing skin. Regular dipping over a period of several weeks will be required to rid your dog of this disquieting condition. Again, steroids may be needed to relieve the itching.

Demodectic mange, caused by mange mites acquired from the mother, is more serious than sarcoptic mange. Medicated dips and antibiotics are indicated, but treatment must be started early if it is to be successful. Symptoms are hair loss around the eyes and on the face, usually in dogs under one year of age.

Internal Parasites

WORMS

Roundworms, which live in the intestinal tract, commonly are found in puppies and should not be cause for alarm unless they are allowed to go untreated. Puppies usually get roundworms from their mothers and may pass them in their stool or, if severely infected, may vomit them up. Although roundworms, which look like moving spaghetti, do not present a serious threat to adult dogs, they can be fatal to young puppies if ignored.

but any litters produced will not be eligible for AKC registration, thereby decreasing their monetary value.

At what age should the surgery be performed? In recent years, the American Veterinary Medical Association has endorsed early spaying/ neutering, as young as eight weeks. This question should be discussed with your own veterinarian and a mutually acceptable decision made.

Sterilization will be beneficial to your dog's health. With males, neutering may effect some positive behavior changes as well. A spayed bitch is not in danger of contracting uterine or ovarian cancer, and the danger of mammary cancer is minimized. The possibility of your bitch getting pyometra, an extremely dangerous uterine infection, is also eliminated.

Neutering the male dog eliminates the possibility of testicular cancer and reduces the chance of prostate problems later in life. In addition, if neutering is done at an early age it may help curb some aggressiveness, though training is a more effective answer to this problem.

The old wives' tales about the effects of spaying and neutering should be discarded. Altering a dog will not cause obesity and laziness; overfeeding and lack of exercise will. Neither males nor females require the experience of breeding to fulfill their lives. They're perfectly happy being your companion and do not need the company of canines of the opposite sex.

A FIRST-AID KIT

Keep a canine first-aid kit on hand for general care and emergencies. Check it periodically to make sure liquids haven't spilled or dried up, and replace medications and materials after they're used. Your kit should include:

Activated charcoal tablets

Adhesive tape
(1 and 2 inches wide)

Antibacterial ointment
(for skin and eyes)

Aspirin (buffered or enteric coated, *not* Ibuprofen)

Bandages: Gauze rolls (1 and 2 inches wide) and dressing pads

Cotton balls

Diarrhea medicine

Dosing syringe

Hydrogen peroxide (3%)

Petroleum jelly

Rectal thermometer

Rubber gloves

Rubbing alcohol

Scissors

Tourniquet

Towel

Tweezers

Intact females generally come in heat twice a year and remain in heat about three weeks. This, by itself, is a good enough reason to spay your bitch. During heat cycles, you'll be attended by an eager clan of males dogs outside your house. You will also have to deal with the inconvenience of the bloody discharge accompanying the heat cycle, either by keeping your pet outfitted with sanitary panties or napkins, or by constantly cleaning up after her.

Even if your precautions with a bitch in heat are successful and no accidental breeding occurs, many females will follow their season by going into a false pregnancy, giving every sign of being bred, including developing milk.

The intact male, once he gets a whiff of a bitch in season, can become totally obnoxious, howling, whining and fasting for up to the entire three-week period.

The best—and only—cure for these inconveniences is altering your pet at a young age.

First-Aid Kit

A doggie first-aid kit is an inexpensive yet valuable acquisition for any dog owner to have available at home and when traveling with a pet. Basic components should in-clude a rectal thermometer (a dog's normal temperature should be just over 101 degrees but can range from 100 to 102.5 degrees Fahrenheit), an antibiotic first aid cream, antihistamine to combat insect stings, buffered aspirin, ear cleanser and/or ointment, bandaging materials, tweezers and alcohol for removing ticks, cotton swabs, peroxide, antiseptic soap, antacid and anti-diarrhea medication.

With these supplies, you can deal with most minor emergencies without rushing your dog to the veterinarian for every bump, bruise and scrape.

Emergency Management

It is important to know what constitutes an emergency and what ailments can be safely dealt with by you at home. In some emergency situations, you will need to administer preliminary treatment before your dog arrives at the vet's. The following information is not meant to substitute for a veterinarian's advice. If you have any concerns, do not hesitate to call.

Use a scarf or old hose to make a temporary muzzle, as shown.

When you call your vet's office in an emergency, try to have as much information on your Basset's condition as possible. The vet will be able to offer advice and treatment more quickly and effectively.

Muzzle   Any injured and frightened dog, even your own, may bite while you're trying to assist him. A piece of cloth, a leash or a pair of pantyhose will serve the purpose of a makeshift muzzle. Start from the underside of the jaw and wrap the material to the top of the muzzle. Tie a knot on top and then bring the material back down underneath the jaw. Tie another knot and then wrap the ends of the muzzle around the neck at the back of the head and tie it securely.

Taking Your Basset's Temperature   One of the most indispensable items you have in your first-aid kit is a rectal thermometer. When you call the veterinarian's office in an emergency, it will aid him or her greatly to know if your dog has a temperature, and if so, how high.

Taking your dog's temperature is easiest if you have a helper to comfort the dog and hold his body firmly so he can't squirm. Shake the thermometer down and coat it with petroleum jelly. Lift your Basset's tail and insert the thermometer about an inch. Don't let go of it! Hold the thermometer as you watch the clock. After three minutes, remove the thermometer, wipe it with a cloth and read the temperature. A dog's normal temperature is between 101 and 102 degrees Fahrenheit. If you feel uncomfortable attempting this procedure, ask your vet to show you how to do it first.

Choking   If a foreign object—usually a bone—becomes lodged in your dog's throat, you may be able to remove it quickly and efficiently by grasping the jaws, opening the mouth and inserting your fingers down the throat. If this is unsuccessful, place the dog on its side, with the head lowered, and put pressure just beneath the rib cage. If this too fails, no time should be lost in getting veterinary help for your pet. En route, preferably with an assistant, keep the air passage open and the tongue pulled to one side.

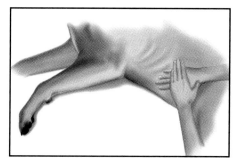

Applying abdominal thrusts can save a choking dog.

Diarrhea   There are numerous reasons why dogs get diarrhea. Improper diet (including the ingestion of foreign objects), a food allergy, illness (either minor or serious), worms and stress all may be contributing factors. In addition to pinpointing the cause, it is essential to prevent your dog from dehydrating during this period of distress. Since puppies dehydrate rather quickly, diarrhea in a youngster requires early veterinary intervention.

With an adult dog, having your veterinarian check a stool sample will help determine if the problem is caused by worms, but meanwhile diarrhea should be treated symptomatically in order to prevent dehydration. Your veterinarian can dispense or recommend a good anti-diarrhea medication. At the same time, dog food should be abandoned temporarily in favor of a bland diet consisting of cooked rice or cottage cheese combined with boiled hamburger or chicken.

Assuming you are dealing with a minor upset and not a major illness such as parvovirus, once the diarrhea clears up you should continue the bland diet for another forty-eight hours. Then *gradually* reintroduce dog food, a very small amount at a time.

In extreme cases of diarrhea, your dog may need to be hospitalized and put on intravenous fluids to overcome dehydration.

Stings In addition to being painful, bee or wasp stings can be extremely dangerous if your dog is allergic. Among the emergency items in your first-aid kit is an antihistamine that should be administered to a dog in distress from an insect sting. The tweezers in your kit can be used to remove a stinger that might be left behind by a bee.

Animal Bites If your Basset gets bitten by another animal, staunch the bleeding with direct pressure to the wound. Pour hydrogen peroxide over the bite to cleanse it. If the bite looks large or the bleeding persists, get your dog to the vet immediately where the vet can stitch it. Make sure the other animal was not rabid. If you have any suspicion that it was, tell your vet.

Run your hands regularly over your dog to feel for any injuries.

Heat Stroke or Heat Prostration If your dog should be overcome by heat, immediate action is necessary to avoid brain damage or death. Immerse the dog in cold water immediately, all the time monitoring his temperature to make sure it is returning to normal. In many cases, the heat will cause some blood vessels to burst, requiring additional medical attention. Once on-the-spot first aid has been provided, the dog should be wrapped in cold towels and taken to the veterinarian as soon as possible.

Heat problems most often are the result of a dog being left in an automobile during the summer months, which should never be done, even with the windows open. Extreme stress also can cause a dog to experience heat stroke.

Hypothermia Exposure to extreme cold can cause a dangerous drop in body temperature, and/or frostbite. A dog suffering from hypothermia should be wrapped in blankets and kept as warm as possible during the emergency trip to the veterinarian.

Poisoning   Many common household substances can be poisonous to your dog. One of the most dangerous is antifreeze, which dogs seem to like the taste of. There are now brands available without the toxic ingredient etheneglycol that offer a safer option for homes with dogs and children. Many houseplants can also be poisonous if ingested. Indoor plants you may want to replace or store in a room your dog does not have access to include amaryllis, ivy and umbrella plant, among others. Toxic outdoor plants include daffodil, azalea, periwinkle, morning glory and larkspur. Consult your local poison control center for a more complete list of dangerous substances around the home and yard.

Some of the many household substances harmful to your dog.

If you know, or suspect, that your dog has ingested poison, you have two immediate options: Contact your own veterinarian or, if after hours, call the Animal Poison Control Center, a twenty-four-hour telephone service that will provide you with information on the toxicity of the ingested substance and advise you on how to get your dog through this crisis. The number for the Animal Poison Control Center, which accepts credit cards for payment, is (800) 962-1253.

Your dog's system will respond to different poisons in different ways. Common symptoms of poisoning include: vomiting, diarrhea, salivation, labored breathing, weakness, convulsions or collapse. Try to determine the kind of poison your dog ingested so the poison control center operator or veterinarian will be able to provide diagnosis and treatment more quickly and effectively. *Do not make your dog vomit unless instructed to do so.*

Trauma   The injured dog should be handled with extreme caution, both for your protection and his. If possible, don heavy-duty gloves before attempting to handle an injured dog. Even your own pet, if hurt and frightened badly enough, may bite under such circumstances. To avoid further injury to the animal, devise a stretcher from a slab of wood or other strong substance and gently move the dog onto it. If nothing else is available, a sheet or large towel will suffice. Use a leash or belt to secure the dog to the makeshift stretcher. Immediate veterinary care is necessary not only for the possible injuries but for shock as well.

Make a tempo-rary splint by wrapping the leg in firm casing, then bandaging it.

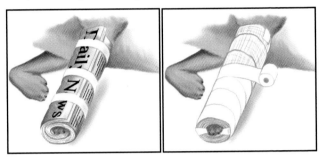

Bleeding   To control bleeding, first you must deter-mine the source, artery or vein. Bright red, spurting blood comes from an artery. Veins seep out blood that is dark red in color. Pressure should be applied to the area to stop venal bleeding. An artery injury requires a tourniquet, applied between the wound and the heart. Wrap a cloth or bandage loosely around the limb and tighten it with a stick or pencil until the bleeding stops. Make sure you loosen it at least at half-hour intervals to allow the blood to flow to the affected area.

In Basset Hounds, the most common bleeding injury is to the ears. This also can be the most difficult area in which to control the bleeding because of the dog's ten-dency to shake its head and restart the bleeding. Though torn ears rarely if ever are life-threatening, they can make your home or car look like a slaughter-house, and often will need suturing.

Anal Glands   If your dog scoots along the floor and bites at his rear end, it could be a sign of impacted, or clogged, anal glands. (This also could indicate the presence of worms.) The anal sacs, which could become infected if not tended to, are located on the two lower sides of the anus, and take on an oval shape when impacted. To express them, cover the area with paper toweling and, starting from the bottom, move upwards toward the anal opening.

The liquid that will be expressed has a nasty odor and should be gray or brown. If the liquid is bloody, consult your veterinarian. If this procedure is more than you can handle, veterinarians and most groomers will do it for you, but do make sure it's not neglected.

Vomiting Like diarrhea, vomiting is usually the result of your Basset having eaten something he shouldn't. If, however, the vomitus is bloody or other-wise unusual, if your dog has other symptoms, including lethargy or fever, or if the vomiting persists, consult your veterinarian immediately.

To give your Basset a pill, place it far into the back of the throat and hold the dog's mouth closed until he appears to have swallowed.

Administering Medicine
TO GIVE A PILL

To administer pills or capsules, grasp your dog's muzzle from the top to open the mouth, and push the skin from the upper jaw into the dog's mouth as a means of keeping the mouth open. With your other hand, shove the pill as far back as possible, using your index finger to push it down the throat. With most breeds, getting a pill far back on the tongue will suffice. Basset Hounds, however, are expert at hiding pills in their jowls and spitting them out when you turn away. Once you feel the pill has been placed almost down the throat, remove your hand and hold the dog's mouth closed until it appears the dog has swallowed. Even then, don't look away for several seconds because your hound still may spit it out. If he does, simply start the process all over again.

If this procedure is too difficult, or if your dog is determined not to take his medicine, you can resort to wrapping pills in a delicacy, such as cheese or bologna.

LIQUID MEDICATION

To administer liquid medication, use a syringe, available from your veterinarian or a drugstore. Make a pocket at the side of the dog's lips and squirt the medicine in, holding the mouth closed until he swallows.

OINTMENT

Applying ointment to your Basset's skin is just the same as applying it to your own, only he's hairier. Part the hair and spread the medication gently around the area as best you can.

*Squeeze eye oint-
ment into the
lower lid.*

For skin conditions, your vet may prescribe an Elizabethan collar along with medicated ointment. These devices, named after the fashionable collar of Elizabeth I's reign, are designed to keep your dog from licking and bothering the infected area. Your dog will most likely hate this contraption, and will do his best to paw and shake it off, but try to get him to keep it on. Otherwise, the wound may take a long while to heal, and can even become badly infected.

Problems Specific to Bassets

The Basset Hound generally is a hardy breed, but like all breeds can be prone to certain ailments, injuries and genetic problems. For your own protection as well as your pet's, you should be familiar with the conditions that might affect the Basset Hound as a puppy or an adult. Your breeder may have discussed some of these conditions with you. You and your veterinarian both should be forewarned so you know what to look for if any symptoms occur. Also, don't hesitate to call the breeder for advice about any health issues.

Eye Disorders

Ectropion An eversion of the eyelid, ectropion is associated with excessive eyelid length and poor eyelid tone. Ophthalmic ointment may be used to reduce irritation, but more severe cases probably will require surgery.

Gland Prolapse Commonly known as "cherry eye," it is easily detected because a pink mass will show up in the eye. This usually occurs in puppies between the ages of six weeks and one year. Manual replacement may be attempted, but surgery usually is called for, preferably to replace the gland and secure it in position. If this fails, partial removal of the gland may be necessary.

Glaucoma The most serious of the eye ailments common to Basset Hounds, this disease may be treated medically if the case is mild, and vision may be saved. In more severe cases, blindness probably will be the end result.

The sightless Basset Hound benefits from his keen sense of smell, which compensates very efficiently for the eyesight loss. He can learn quickly to find his way around in familiar surroundings. We once took in a dog whose owner would not or could not cope with the dog's glaucoma-induced blindness. In short order, he learned his way around his new environment. As long as we followed the identical route for his walks he knew exactly where he was going, where the steps were and the location of every tree worth marking. He lived out his life with us, none the worse for his sightlessness.

> ### WHEN TO CALL THE VET
>
> In any emergency situation, you should call your veterinarian immediately. You can make the difference in your dog's life by staying as calm as possible when you call and by giving the doctor or the assistant as much information as possible before you leave for the clinic. That way, the vet will be able to take immediate, specific action to remedy your dog's situation.
>
> Emergencies include acute abdominal pain, suspected poisoning, snakebite, burns, frostbite, shock, dehydration, abnormal vomiting or bleeding, and deep wounds. You are the best judge of your dog's health, as you live with and observe him every day. Don't hesitate to call your veterinarian if you suspect trouble.

Conjunctivitis   This inflammation of the third eyelid or the tissues lining the lids is caused by a collection of dirt, pollen, dust and the variety of other foreign objects that tend to gather in the eyes of a dog whose nose is to the ground. Eye wash can soothe the condition but veterinary attention is generally needed.

Eye Injuries   Corneal scratches and other injuries require immediate veterinary attention if the vision is to be saved.

SKELETAL PROBLEMS

As a "dwarf," or chondrodystrophic breed, the Basset Hound is prone to a number of orthopedic ailments that owners and veterinarians alike should be aware of.

The Basset Hound eye can be prone to problems, though his keen sense of smell compensates for any reduced vision he may experience.

Panosteitis   An inflammation of the long bones, panosteitis generally occurs between the ages of six months and two years. It is characterized by a sudden onset of lameness, usually starting in the front legs but possibly shifting from leg to leg. Fever may accompany the lameness. Because some veterinary manuals fail to list the Basset Hound as being among the breeds afflicted with panosteitis, you may need to inform your doctor that this, indeed, is a Basset Hound ailment. Radio-graphs will diagnose pano, and the accepted treatment is rest, time and, if necessary, an analgesic for pain.

Osteochondritis   Dessicans This condition of the shoulder is caused by cartilage trauma and results in severe lameness, usually seen in dogs between the ages of six months and two years. Extensive rest may be of help, but surgery may be needed to repair the damage caused by detached cartilage.

Injuries to the Stifle (Knee)   These also are relatively common among Basset Hounds and usually are caused by a ruptured ligament. With total rest, the dog may be able to put weight on the knee, but surgery will bring about more stability and a longer-range cure.

Patella, or Kneecap, Luxation This affects the hind legs, with the kneecap slipping to one side as a result of defective grooves or ridges. This generally will surface after the age of six months, and can be repaired through surgery.

Elbow Dysplasia Caused by failure of the ulna to become normal bone, elbow dysplasia results in a piece of loose bone in the elbow joint. The loose bone must be removed surgically to alleviate the lameness.

Herniated Discs If left untreated, herniated discs can result in total paralysis. Disc problems, relatively common to all long-backed dogs, may be caused by a trauma or, according to some orthopedic specialists, "just happen." Mild cases may be treated with steroids; more severe incidents will require almost immediate surgery.

Hip Dysplasia A number of veterinarians have misdiagnosed hip dysplasia in Basset Hounds, failing to take into consideration the breed's unusual bone structure. Because of this structure, it would be virtually impossible for a Basset Hound to develop what would be considered "normal" hips in a traditional breed of dog. The actual incidence of hip dysplasia in Basset Hounds is very low, according to the experts at the Orthopedic Foundation for Animals and other orthopedic specialists worldwide.

An Elizabethan collar keeps your dog from licking a fresh wound.

Other Ailments

von Willebrand's Disease This is a bleeding disorder that interferes with the clotting mechanism and could result in severe hemorrhage from a minor injury or during surgery. Testing can detect whether a dog suffers from this inherited disorder.

Inguinal Hernias These hernias are life-threatening if not treated surgically at once. Abdominal organs or fat in the groin swell, shutting off the blood supply. Peritonitis is the result if quick surgical measures are not taken to prevent strangulation.

Urinary Tract Disorders Although such disorders can occur in any breed, some Basset Hounds seem especially prone. Stone formation in the kidney or urinary bladder is caused by excessive excretion of cystine, an amino acid. Prescription diets may dis-

solve the stones, or surgery will be required. Simple urinary tract infections start with excessive water con-sumption and frequent urination, often accompanied by straining and/or blood in the urine. The appropriate antibiotic will clear up the problem in two to three weeks.

With your special care, the older Basset Hound will still get a lot of enjoyment from life.

Torsion As mentioned in chapter 5, bloat, or dilatation and torsion of the stomach, can occur in Basset Hounds as well as in other deep-chested breeds. Prompt treatment is necessary if the animal is to survive. Symptoms are distention of the abdomen, attempts to vomit and obvious distress. A tube may be inserted into the stomach to relieve the gas if the stomach has not yet twisted. Once the stomach twists, surgery is required. The dog also must be treated for shock.

Sebaceous Gland Tumors These tumors in the skin are common in Basset Hounds and can often go untreated. However, if they become enlarged or ulcerated, surgery may be necessary.

The Senior Citizen

Despite your best efforts to keep your dog healthy and fit, the day will come when you realize your companion has slowed down just a tad and doesn't have quite the lilt to his walk that he once had. The geriatric dog requires special care and relies on you to provide it.

DIET

As your dog ages and his activity level slows, a "less active" diet will be needed to avoid obesity and still provide the necessary nutrients. Choose the "senior" formula of the kibble you've been feeding him.

EXERCISE

Your Basset will walk more slowly as he ages, but it is still important to take him for a brief walk around the neighborhood. Aside from being given the opportunity to relieve himself, he needs the stimulation that seeing and smelling the world around him provides.

PHYSICAL CHANGES

Your older Basset's senses will not be as sharp as they were when he was an alert pup; he may not hear or see as well, and his reflexes may not be as sharp as they once were. He may become more sensitive to heat and cold, and less tolerant of rambunctious children and puppies and changes in his routine.

Do everything you can to keep your older Basset comfortable. Keep a cozy bed available away from drafts, and be patient with his slowness and stiff movement. If you call him and he doesn't respond, call a little louder; he probably just doesn't hear you.

Arthritis is fairly common in the older dog, and Basset Hounds are particularly prone to this painful affliction because of their odd bone structure. An occasional buffered aspirin will help the average arthritic dog cope with the aches and pains, but in more extreme cases, and particularly when cold and/or wet weather prevails for an extended period, other measures may be needed. Steroids often are used to reduce inflammation and pain, but the side effects from extended use could be more devastating than the disease itself. Ask your vet about the nonsteroid products now on the market that reduce inflammation without doing their own mischief.

When the End Comes . . .

With every pet, the day comes when we must say good-bye. Barring illness or accident, you may be faced with deciding when that day has arrived. A veterinarian told me many years ago that I would know when my beloved dog no longer was enjoying his life. "Let him go while he still has his dignity," he advised me.

You, too, will know when that day comes and you must make the dreaded appointment with your veterinarian. There are alternatives, but they are far less humane than accompanying your pet, comforting him and assuring him of your love during those final minutes. I have seen pet owners take their aged "best friends" into their local shelter or pound and leave them there, alone and frightened, to be euthanized in the company of total strangers. I cannot imagine a more cruel way to close out the years of loyalty and friendship that go with dog ownership.

Check your dog's teeth frequently and brush them regularly.

Coping with the sorrow of pet loss is a very individual situation. Many shelters and veterinary schools have counselors and group sessions available to help bereaved pet owners work through this crisis. The mourning period differs for each of us, but when it ends it's time to go on to the next phase of your life, which usually involves getting a *new* dog, never a *replacement*.

With that decision, the excitement and pleasure begin all over again, along with the challenge of raising another physically and mentally sound companion who will be with you for many happy years.

Your Happy, Healthy Pet

Your Dog's Name _____

Name on Your Dog's Pedigree (if your dog has one) _____

_____

Where Your Dog Came From _____

_____

Your Dog's Birthday _____

Your Dog's Veterinarian

    Name _____

    Address _____

    Phone Number_____

    Emergency Number_____

Your Dog's Health

    Vaccines

    type _____ date given _____

    type _____ date given _____

    type _____ date given _____

    type _____ date given _____

    Heartworm

    date tested _____ type used_____ start date _____

Your Dog's License Number_____

Groomer's Name and Number _____

Dogsitter/Walker's Name and Number_____

Awards Your Dog Has Won

    Award _____ date earned _____

    Award _____ date earned _____

part three

Enjoying
your
Dog

chapter 8

Basic
Training

by Ian Dunbar, Ph.D., MRCVS

Training is the jewel in the crown—the most important aspect of doggy husbandry. There is no more important variable influencing dog behavior and temperament than the dog's education: A well-trained, well-behaved and good-natured puppydog is always a joy to live with, but an untrained and uncivilized dog can be a perpetual nightmare. Moreover, deny the dog an education and it will not have the opportunity to fulfill its own canine potential; neither will it have the ability to communicate effectively with its human companions.

Luckily, modern psychological training methods are easy, efficient and effective and, above all, considerably dog-friendly and user-friendly. Doggy education is as simple as it is enjoyable. But before you can have a good time play-training with your new dog, you have to learn what to do and how to do it. There is no bigger variable influencing the success of dog training than the *owner's* experience and expertise. *Before you embark on the dog's education, you must first educate yourself.*

Basic Training for Owners

Ideally, basic owner training should begin well *before* you select your dog. Find out all you can about your chosen breed first, then master rudimentary training and handling skills. If you already have your puppy/dog, owner training is a dire emergency—the clock is running! Especially for puppies, the first few weeks at home are the most important and influential days in the dog's life. Indeed, the cause of most adolescent and adult problems may be traced back to the initial days the pup explores his new home. This is the time to establish the *status quo*—to teach the puppy/dog how you would like him to behave and so prevent otherwise quite predictable problems.

In addition to consulting breeders and breed books such as this one (which understandably have a positive breed bias), seek out as many pet owners with your breed you can find. Good points are obvious. What you want to find out are the breed-specific *problems*, so you can nip them in the bud. In particular, you should talk to owners with *adolescent* dogs and make a list of all anticipated problems. Most important, *test drive* at least half a dozen adolescent and adult dogs of your breed yourself. An eight-week-old puppy is deceptively easy to handle, but she will acquire adult size, speed and strength in just four months, so you should learn now what to prepare for.

Puppy and pet dog training classes offer a convenient venue to locate pet owners and observe dogs in action. For a list of suitable trainers in your area, contact the Association of Pet Dog Trainers (see Chapter 13). You may also begin your basic owner training by observing other owners in class. Watch as many classes and test drive as many dogs as possible. Select an upbeat, dog-friendly, people-friendly, fun-and-games, puppydog pet training class to learn the ropes. Also, watch training videos and read training books (see Chapter 12). You must find out what to do and how to do it *before* you have to do it.

Principles of Training

Most people think training comprises teaching the dog to do things such as sit, speak and roll over, but even a four-week-old pup knows how to do these things already. Instead, the first step in training involves teaching the dog human words for each dog behavior and activity and for each aspect of the dog's environment. That way you, the owner, can more easily participate in the dog's domestic education by directing him to perform specific actions appropriately, that is, at the right time, in the right place, and so on. Training opens communication channels, enabling an educated dog to at least understand the owner's requests.

In addition to teaching a dog *what* we want her to do, it is also necessary to teach her *why* she should do what we ask. Indeed, 95 percent of training revolves around motivating the dog *to want to do* what we want. Dogs often understand what their owners want; they just don't see the point of doing it—especially when the owner's repetitively boring and seemingly senseless instructions are totally at odds with much more pressing and exciting doggy distractions. It is not so much the dog who is being stubborn or dominant; rather, it is the owner who has failed to acknowledge the dog's needs and feelings and to approach training from the dog's point of view.

The Meaning of Instructions

The secret to successful training is learning how to use training lures to predict or prompt specific behaviors—to coax the dog to do what you want *when* you want. Any highly valued object (such as a treat or toy) may be used as a lure, which the dog will follow with his eyes and nose. Moving the lure in specific ways entices the dog to move his nose, head and entire body in specific ways. In fact, by learning the art of manipulating various lures, it is possible to teach the dog to assume virtually any body position and perform any action. Once you have control over the expression of the dog's behaviors and can elicit any body position or behavior at will, you can easily teach the dog to perform on request.

Tell your dog what you want him to do, use a lure to entice him to respond correctly, then profusely praise

Teach your dog words for each activity he needs to know, like down.

and maybe reward him once he performs the desired action. For example, verbally request "Fido, sit!" while you move a squeaky toy upwards and backwards over the dog's muzzle (lure-movement and hand signal), smile knowingly as he looks up (to follow the lure) and sits down (as a result of canine anatomical engineering), then praise him to distraction ("Gooood Fido!"). Squeak the toy, offer a training treat and give your dog and yourself a pat on the back.

Being able to elicit desired responses over and over enables the owner to reward the dog over and over. Consequently, the dog begins to think training is fun. For example, the more the dog is rewarded for sitting, the more she enjoys sitting. Eventually the dog comes to realize that, whereas most sitting is appreciated, sitting immediately upon request usually prompts especially enthusiastic praise and a slew of high-level rewards. The dog begins to sit on cue much of the time, showing that she is starting to grasp the meaning of the owner's verbal request and hand signal.

Why Comply?

Most dogs enjoy initial lure/reward training and are only too happy to comply with their owners' wishes. Unfortunately, repetitive drilling without appreciative feedback tends to diminish the dog's enthusiasm until he eventually fails to see the point of complying anymore. Moreover, as the dog approaches adolescence he becomes more easily distracted as he develops other interests. Lengthy sessions with repetitive exercises tend to bore and demotivate both parties. If it's not fun, the owner doesn't do it and neither does the dog.

Integrate training into your dog's life: The greater number of training sessions each day and the *shorter* they are, the more willingly compliant your dog will become. Make sure to have a short (just a few seconds) training interlude before every enjoyable canine activity. For example, ask your dog to sit to greet people, to sit before you throw his Frisbee, and to sit for his supper. Really, sitting is no different from a canine "please." Also, include numerous short training interludes during every enjoyable canine pastime, for example, when playing with the dog or when he is running in the park. In this fashion, doggy distractions may be effectively converted into rewards for training. Just as all games have rules, fun becomes training . . . and training becomes fun.

Eventually, rewards actually become unnecessary to continue motivating your dog. If trained with consideration and kindness, performing the desired behaviors will become self-rewarding and, in a sense, your dog will motivate himself. Just as it is not necessary to reward a human companion during an enjoyable walk in the park, or following a game of tennis, it is hardly necessary to reward our best friend—the dog—for walking by our side or while playing fetch. Human

company during enjoyable activities is reward enough for most dogs.

Even though your dog has become self-motivating, it's still good to praise and pet him a lot and offer rewards once in a while, especially for a good job well done. And if for no other reason, praising and rewarding others is good for the human heart.

To train your dog, you need gentle hands, a loving heart and a good attitude.

Punishment

Without a doubt, lure/reward training is by far the best way to teach: Entice your dog to do what you want and then reward him for doing so. Unfortunately, a human shortcoming is to take the good for granted and to moan and groan at the bad. Specifically, the dog's many good behaviors are ignored while the owner focuses on punishing the dog for making mistakes. In extreme cases, instruction is *limited* to punishing mistakes made by a trainee dog, child, employee or husband, even though it has been proven punishment training is notoriously inefficient and ineffective and is decidedly unfriendly and combative. It teaches the dog that training is a drag, almost as quickly as it teaches the dog to dislike his trainer. Why treat our best friends like our worst enemies?

Punishment training is also much more laborious and time consuming. Whereas it takes only a finite amount of time to teach a dog what to chew, for example, it takes much, much longer to punish the dog for each and every mistake. Remember, *there is only one right way!* So why not teach that right way from the outset?!

103

To make matters worse, punishment training causes severe lapses in the dog's reliability. Since it is obviously impossible to punish the dog each and every time she misbehaves, the dog quickly learns to distinguish between those times when she must comply (so as to avoid impending punishment) and those times when she need not comply, because punishment is impossible. Such times include when the dog is off leash and only six feet away, when the owner is otherwise engaged (talking to a friend, watching television, taking a shower, tending to the baby or chatting on the telephone), or when the dog is left at home alone.

Instances of misbehavior will be numerous when the owner is away, because even when the dog complied in the owner's looming presence, he did so unwillingly. The dog was forced to act against his will, rather than moulding his will to want to please. Hence, when the owner is absent, not only does the dog know he need not comply, he simply does not want to. Again, the trainee is not a stubborn vindictive beast, but rather the trainer has failed to teach.

Punishment training invariably creates unpredictable Jekyll and Hyde behavior.

Trainer's Tools

Many training books extol the virtues of a vast array of training paraphernalia and electronic and metallic gizmos, most of which are designed for canine restraint, correction and punishment, rather than for actual facilitation of doggy education. In reality, most effective training tools are not found in stores; they come from within ourselves. In addition to a willing dog, all you really need is a functional human brain, gentle hands, a loving heart and a good attitude.

In terms of equipment, all dogs do require a quality buckle collar to sport dog tags and to attach the leash (for safety and to comply with local leash laws). Hollow chewtoys (like Kongs or sterilized longbones) and a dog bed or collapsible crate are a must for housetraining. Three additional tools are required:

1. specific lures (training treats and toys) to predict and prompt specific desired behaviors;

2. rewards (praise, affection, training treats and toys) to reinforce for the dog what a lot of fun it all is; and

3. knowledge—how to convert the dog's favorite activities and games (potential distractions to training) into "life-rewards," which may be employed to facilitate training.

The most powerful of these is *knowledge*. Education is the key! Watch training classes, participate in training classes, watch videos, read books, enjoy playtraining with your dog, and then your dog will say "Please," and your dog will say "Thank you!"

Housetraining

If dogs were left to their own devices, certainly they would chew, dig and bark for entertainment and then no doubt highlight a few areas of their living space with sprinkles of urine, in much the same way we decorate by hanging pictures. Consequently, when we ask a dog to live with us, we must teach him *where* he may dig and perform his toilet duties, *what* he may chew and *when* he may bark. After all, when left at home alone for many hours, we cannot expect the dog to amuse himself by completing crosswords or watching the soaps on TV!

Also, it would be decidedly unfair to keep the house rules a secret from the dog, and then get angry and punish the poor critter for inevitably transgressing rules he did not even know existed. Remember, without adequate education and guidance, the dog will be forced to establish his own rules—doggy rules—that most probably will be at odds with the owner's view of domestic living.

Since most problems develop during the first few days the dog is at home, prospective dog owners must be certain they are quite clear about the principles of housetraining *before* they get a dog. Early misbehaviors quickly become established as the status quo—

becoming firmly entrenched as hard-to-break bad habits, which set the precedent for years to come. Make sure to teach your dog good habits right from the start. Good habits are just as hard to break as bad ones!

Ideally, when a new dog comes home, try to arrange for someone to be present for as much as possible during the first few days (for adult dogs) or weeks for puppies. With only a little forethought, it is surprisingly easy to find a puppy sitter, such as a retired person, who would be willing to eat from your refrigerator and watch your television while keeping an eye on the newcomer to encourage the dog to play with chewtoys and to ensure he goes outside on a regular basis.

POTTY TRAINING

To teach the dog where to relieve himself:

1. never let him make a single mistake;

2. let him know where you want him to go; and

3. handsomely reward him for doing so: "GOOOOOOOD DOG!!!" liver treat, liver treat, liver treat!

PREVENTING MISTAKES

A single mistake is a training disaster, since it heralds many more in future weeks. And each time the dog soils the house, this further reinforces the dog's unfortunate preference for an indoor, carpeted toilet. *Do not let an unhousetrained dog have full run of the house if you are away from home or cannot pay full attention.* Instead, confine the dog to an area where elimination is appropriate, such as an outdoor run or, better still, a small, comfortable indoor kennel with access to an outdoor run. When confined in this manner, most dogs will naturally housetrain themselves.

If that's not possible, confine the dog to an area, such as a utility room, kitchen, basement or garage, where elimination may not be desired in the long run but as an interim measure it is certainly preferable to doing it all around the house. Use newspaper to cover the floor of the dog's day room. The newspaper may be used to soak up the urine and to wrap up and dispose of the feces. Once your dog develops a preferred spot for eliminating, it is only necessary to cover that part of the floor with newspaper. The smaller papered area may then be moved (only a little each day) towards the door to the outside. Thus the dog will develop the tendency to go to the door when he needs to relieve himself.

Never confine an unhousetrained dog to a crate for long periods. Doing so would force the dog to soil the crate and ruin its usefulness as an aid for housetraining (see the following discussion).

The first few weeks at home are the most important and influential in your dog's life.

TEACHING WHERE

In order to teach your dog where you would like her to do her business, you have to be there to direct the proceedings—an obvious, yet often neglected, fact of life. In order to be there to teach the dog *where* to go, you need to know *when* she needs to go. Indeed, the success of housetraining depends on the owner's ability to predict these times. Certainly, a regular feeding schedule will facilitate prediction somewhat, but there is

nothing like "loading the deck" and influencing the timing of the outcome yourself!

Whenever you are at home, make sure the dog is under constant supervision and/or confined to a small

107

area. If already well trained, simply instruct the dog to lie down in his bed or basket. Alternatively, confine the dog to a crate (doggy den) or tie-down (a short, 18-inch lead that can be clipped to an eye hook in the baseboard). Short-term close confinement strongly inhibits urination and defecation, since the dog does not want to soil his sleeping area. Thus, when you release the puppydog each hour, he will definitely need to urinate immediately and defecate every third or fourth hour. Keep the dog confined to his doggy den and take him to his intended toilet area each hour, every hour, and on the hour.

When taking your dog outside, instruct him to sit quietly before opening the door—he will soon learn to sit by the door when he needs to go out!

TEACHING WHY

Being able to predict when the dog needs to go enables the owner to be on the spot to praise and reward the dog. Each hour, hurry the dog to the intended toilet area in the yard, issue the appropriate instruction ("Go pee!" or "Go poop!"), then give the dog three to four minutes to produce. Praise and offer a couple of training treats when successful. The treats are important because many people fail to praise their dogs with feeling . . . and housetraining is hardly the time for understatement. So either loosen up and enthusiastically praise that dog: "Wuzzzer-wuzzer-wuzzer, hoooser good wuffer den? Hoooo went pee for Daddy?" Or say "Good dog!" as best you can and offer the treats for effect.

Following elimination is an ideal time for a spot of playtraining in the yard or house. Also, an empty dog may be allowed greater freedom around the house for the next half hour or so, just as long as you keep an eye out to make sure he does not get into other kinds of mischief. If you are preoccupied and cannot pay full attention, confine the dog to his doggy den once more to enjoy a peaceful snooze or to play with his many chewtoys.

If your dog does not eliminate within the allotted time outside—no biggie! Back to his doggy den, and then try again after another hour.

As I own large dogs, I always feel more relaxed walking an empty dog, knowing that I will not need to finish our stroll weighted down with bags of feces! Beware of falling into the trap of walking the dog to get it to eliminate. The good ol' dog walk is such an enormous highlight in the dog's life that it represents the single biggest potential reward in domestic dogdom. However, when in a hurry, or during inclement weather, many owners abruptly terminate the walk the moment the dog has done its business. This, in effect, severely punishes the dog for doing the right thing, in the right place at the right time. Consequently, many dogs become strongly inhibited from eliminating outdoors because they know it will signal an abrupt end to an otherwise thoroughly enjoyable walk.

Instead, instruct the dog to relieve himself in the yard prior to going for a walk. If you follow the above instructions, most dogs soon learn to eliminate on cue. As soon as the dog eliminates, praise (and offer a treat or two)—"Good dog! Let's go walkies!" Use the walk as a reward for eliminating in the yard. If the dog does not go, put him back in his doggy den and think about a walk later on. You will find with a "No feces–no walk" policy, your dog will become one of the fastest defecators in the business.

If you do not have a back yard, instruct the dog to eliminate right outside your front door prior to the walk. Not only will this facilitate clean up and disposal of the feces in your own trash can but, also, the walk may again be used as a colossal reward.

Chewing and Barking

Short-term close confinement also teaches the dog that occasional quiet moments are a reality of domestic living. Your puppydog is extremely impressionable during his first few weeks at home. Regular confinement at this time soon exerts a calming influence over the dog's personality. Remember, once the dog is housetrained and calmer, there will be a whole lifetime ahead for the dog to enjoy full run of the house and garden. On the other hand, by letting the newcomer have unrestricted access to the entire household and allowing him to run willy-nilly, he will most certainly develop a bunch of behavior problems in short order, no doubt necessitating confinement later in life. It would not be fair to remedially restrain and confine a dog you have trained, through neglect, to run free.

When confining the dog, make sure he always has an impressive array of suitable chewtoys. Kongs and sterilized longbones (both readily available from pet stores) make the best chewtoys, since they are hollow and may be stuffed with treats to heighten the dog's interest. For example, by stuffing the little hole at the top of a Kong with a small piece of freeze-dried liver, the dog will not want to leave it alone.

Remember, treats do not have to be junk food and they certainly should not represent extra calories. Rather, treats should be part of each dog's regular daily diet:

Make sure your puppy has suitable chewtoys.

Some food may be served in the dog's bowl for breakfast and dinner, some food may be used as training treats, and some food may be used for stuffing chewtoys. I regularly stuff my dogs' many Kongs with different shaped biscuits and kibble. The kibble seems to fall out fairly easily, as do the oval-shaped biscuits, thus rewarding the dog instantaneously for checking out the chewtoys. The bone-shaped biscuits fall out after a while, rewarding the dog for worrying at the chewtoy. But the triangular biscuits never come out. They remain inside the Kong as lures, maintaining the dog's fascination with its chewtoy. To further focus the dog's interest, I always make sure to flavor the triangular biscuits by rubbing them with a little cheese or freeze-dried liver.

If stuffed chewtoys are reserved especially for times the dog is confined, the puppydog will soon learn to enjoy quiet moments in her doggy den and she will quickly develop a chewtoy habit—a good habit! This is a simple *passive training* process; all the owner has to do is set up the situation and the dog all but trains herself—easy and effective. Even when the dog is given run of the house, her first inclination will be to indulge her rewarding chewtoy habit rather than destroying less-attractive household articles, such as curtains, carpets, chairs and compact disks. Similarly, a chewtoy chewer will be less inclined to scratch and chew herself excessively. Also, if the dog busies herself as a recreational chewer, she will be less inclined to develop into a recreational barker or digger when left at home alone.

Stuff a number of chewtoys whenever the dog is left confined and remove the extra-special-tasting treats when you return. Your dog will now amuse himself with his chewtoys before falling asleep and then resume playing with his chewtoys when he expects you to return. Since most owner-absent misbehavior happens right after you leave and right before your expected return, your puppydog will now be conveniently preoccupied with his chewtoys at these times.

Come and Sit

Most puppies will happily approach virtually anyone, whether called or not; that is, until they collide with

To teach come, call your dog, open your arms as a welcoming signal, wave a toy or a treat and praise for every step in your direction.

adolescence and develop other more important doggy interests, such as sniffing a multiplicity of exquisite odors on the grass. Your mission, Mr. and/or Ms. Owner, is to teach and reward the pup for coming reliably, willingly and happily when called—and you have just three months to get it done. Unless adequately reinforced, your puppy's tendency to approach people will self-destruct by adolescence.

Call your dog ("Fido, come!"), open your arms (and maybe squat down) as a welcoming signal, waggle a treat or toy as a lure, and reward the puppydog when he comes running. Do not wait to praise the dog until he reaches you—he may come 95 percent of the way and then run off after some distraction. Instead, praise the dog's *first* step towards you and continue praising enthusiastically for *every* step he takes in your direction.

When the rapidly approaching puppy dog is three lengths away from impact, instruct him to sit ("Fido, sit!") and hold the lure in front of you in an outstretched hand to prevent him from hitting you midchest and knocking you flat on your back! As Fido decelerates to nose the lure, move the treat upwards and backwards just over his muzzle with an upwards motion of your extended arm (palm-upwards). As the dog looks up to follow the lure, he will sit down (if he jumps up, you are holding the lure too high). Praise the dog for sitting. Move backwards and call him again. Repeat this many times over, always praising when Fido comes and sits; on occasion, reward him.

For the first couple of trials, use a training treat both as a lure to entice the dog to come and sit and as a reward for doing so. Thereafter, try to use different items as lures and rewards. For example, lure the dog with a Kong or Frisbee but reward her with a food treat. Or lure the dog with a food treat but pat her and throw a tennis ball as a reward. After just a few repetitions, dispense with the lures and rewards; the dog will begin to respond willingly to your verbal requests and hand signals just for the prospect of praise from your heart and affection from your hands.

Instruct every family member, friend and visitor how to get the dog to come and sit. Invite people over for a series of pooch parties; do not keep the pup a secret— let other people enjoy this puppy, and let the pup enjoy other people. Puppydog parties are not only fun, they easily attract a lot of people to help *you* train *your* dog. Unless you teach your dog *how* to meet people, that is, to sit for greetings, no doubt the dog will resort to jumping up. Then you and the visitors will get annoyed, and the dog will be punished. This is not fair. *Send out those invitations for puppy parties and teach your dog to be mannerly and socially acceptable.*

Even though your dog quickly masters obedient recalls in the house, his reliability may falter when playing in the back yard or local park. Ironically, it is *the owner* who has unintentionally trained the dog *not* to respond in these instances. By allowing the dog to play and run around and otherwise have a good time, but then to call the dog to put him on leash to take him home, the dog quickly learns playing is fun but training is a drag. Thus, playing in the park becomes a severe distraction, which works against training. Bad news!

Instead, whether playing with the dog off leash or on leash, request him to come at frequent intervals— say, every minute or so. On most occasions, praise and pet the dog for a few seconds while he is sitting, then tell him to go play again. For especially fast recalls, offer a couple of training treats and take the time to praise and pet the dog enthusiastically before releasing him. The dog will learn that coming when called is not necessarily the end of the play session, and neither is it the end of the world; rather, it signals an enjoyable, quality time-out with the owner before resuming play once more. In fact, playing in the park now becomes a very effective life-reward, which works to facilitate training by reinforcing each obedient and timely recall. Good news!

Sit, Down, Stand and Rollover

Teaching the dog a variety of body positions is easy for owner and dog, impressive for spectators and extremely useful for all. Using lure-reward techniques, it is possible to train several positions at once to verbal commands or hand signals (which impress the socks off onlookers).

Sit and *down*—the two control commands—prevent or resolve nearly a hundred behavior problems. For example, if the dog happily and obediently sits or lies down when requested, he cannot jump on visitors, dash out the front door, run around and chase its tail, pester other dogs, harass cats or annoy family, friends or strangers. Additionally, "sit" or "down" are better emergency commands for off-leash control.

It is easier to teach and maintain a reliable sit than maintain a reliable recall. *Sit* is the purest and simplest of commands—either the dog is sitting or he is not. If there is any change of circumstances or potential danger in the park, for example, simply instruct the dog to sit. If he sits, you have a number of options: allow the dog to resume playing when he is safe; walk up and put the dog on leash, or call the dog. The dog will be much more likely to come when called if he has already acknowledged his compliance by sitting. If the dog does not sit in the park—train him to!

Stand and *rollover-stay* are the two positions for examining the dog. Your veterinarian will love you to distraction if you take a little time to teach the dog to stand still and roll over and play possum. Also, your vet bills will be smaller. The rollover-stay is an especially useful command and is really just a variation of the down-stay: whereas the dog lies prone in the traditional down, she lies supine in the rollover-stay.

As with teaching come and sit, the training techniques to teach the dog to assume all other body positions on cue are user-friendly and dog-friendly. Simply give the appropriate request, lure the dog into the desired body position using a training treat or toy and then *praise* (and maybe reward) the dog as soon as he complies. Try not to touch the dog to get him to respond. If you teach the dog by guiding him into position, the dog will quickly learn that rump-pressure means sit, for example, but as yet you still have no control over your dog if he is just six feet away. It will still be necessary to teach the dog to sit on request. So do not make training a time-consuming two-step process; instead, teach the dog to sit to a verbal request or hand signal from the outset. Once the dog sits willingly when requested, by all means use your hands to pet the dog when he does so.

To teach *down* when the dog is already sitting, say "Fido, down!," hold the lure in one hand (palm down) and lower that hand to the floor between the dog's forepaws. As the dog lowers his head to follow the lure, slowly move the lure away from the dog just a fraction (in front of his paws). The dog will lie down as he stretches his nose forward to follow the lure. Praise the dog when he does so. If the dog stands up, you pulled the lure away too far and too quickly.

When teaching the dog to lie down from the standing position, say "down" and lower the lure to the floor as before. Once the dog has lowered his forequarters and assumed a play bow, gently and slowly move the lure *towards* the dog between his forelegs. Praise the dog as soon as his rear end plops down.

After just a couple of trials it will be possible to alternate sits and downs and have the dog energetically perform doggy push-ups. Praise the dog a lot, and after half a dozen or so push-ups reward the dog with a training treat or toy. You will notice the more energetically you move your arm—upwards (palm up) to get the dog to sit, and downwards (palm down) to get the dog to lie down—the more energetically the dog responds to your requests. Now try training the dog in silence and you will notice he has also learned to respond to hand signals. Yeah! Not too shabby for the first session.

To teach *stand* from the sitting position, say "Fido, stand," slowly move the lure half a dog-length away from the dog's nose, keeping it at nose level, and praise the dog as he stands to follow the lure. As soon

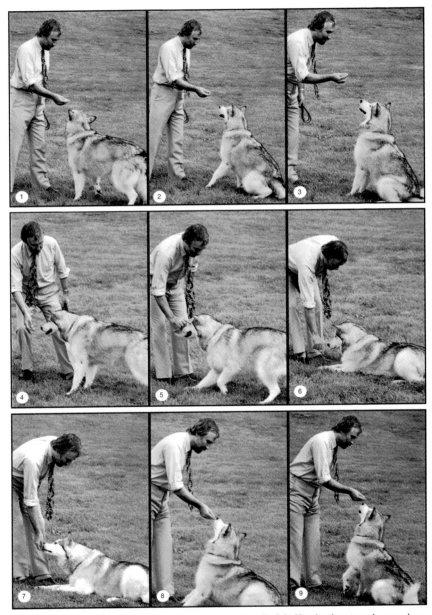

Using a food lure to teach sit, down and stand. 1) "Phoenix, Sit." 2) Hand palm upwards, move lure up and back over dog's muzzle. 3) "Good sit, Phoenix!" 4) "Phoenix, down." 5) Hand palm downwards, move lure down to lie between dog's forepaws. 6) "Phoenix, off. Good down, Phoenix!" 7) "Phoenix, sit!" 8) Palm upwards, move lure up and back, keeping it close to dog's muzzle. 9) "Good sit, Phoenix!"

10) "Phoenix, stand!" 11) Move lure away from dog at nose height, then lower it a tad. 12) "Phoenix, off! Good stand, Phoenix!" 13) "Phoenix, down!" 14) Hand palm downwards, move lure down to lie between dog's forepaws. 15) "Phoenix, off! Good down-stay, Phoenix!" 16) "Phoenix, stand!" 17) Move lure away from dog's muzzle up to nose height. 18) "Phoenix, off! Good stand-stay, Phoenix. Now we'll make the vet and groomer happy!"

as the dog stands, lower the lure to just beneath the dog's chin to entice him to look down; otherwise he will stand and then sit immediately. To prompt the dog to stand from the down position, move the lure half a dog-length upwards and away from the dog, holding the lure at standing nose height from the floor.

Teaching *rollover* is best started from the down position, with the dog lying on one side, or at least with both hind legs stretched out on the same side. Say "Fido, bang!" and move the lure backwards and alongside the dog's muzzle to its elbow (on the side of its outstretched hind legs). Once the dog looks to the side and backwards, very slowly move the lure upwards to the dog's shoulder and backbone. Tickling the dog in the goolies (groin area) often invokes a reflex-raising of the hind leg as an appeasement gesture, which facilitates the tendency to roll over. If you move the lure too quickly and the dog jumps into the standing position, have patience and start again. As soon as the dog rolls onto its back, keep the lure stationary and mesmerize the dog with a relaxing tummy rub.

To teach *rollover-stay* when the dog is standing or moving, say "Fido, bang!" and give the appropriate hand signal (with index finger pointed and thumb cocked in true Sam Spade fashion), then in one fluid movement lure him to first lie down and then rollover-stay as above.

Teaching the dog to *stay* in each of the above four positions becomes a piece of cake after first teaching the dog not to worry at the toy or treat training lure. This is best accomplished by hand feeding dinner kibble. Hold a piece of kibble firmly in your hand and softly instruct "Off!" Ignore any licking and slobbering *for however long the dog worries at the treat*, but say "Take it!" and offer the kibble *the instant* the dog breaks contact with his muzzle. Repeat this a few times, and then up the ante and insist the dog remove his muzzle for one whole second before offering the kibble. Then progressively refine your criteria and have the dog not touch your hand (or treat) for longer and longer periods on each trial, such as for two seconds, four seconds, then six, ten, fifteen, twenty, thirty seconds and so on. The dog soon learns: (1) worrying at the treat never gets results, whereas (2) noncontact is often rewarded after a variable time lapse.

Teaching *"Off!"* has many useful applications in its own right. Additionally, instructing the dog not to touch a training lure often produces spontaneous and magical stays. Request the dog to stand-stay, for example, and not to touch the lure. At first set your sights on a short two-second stay before rewarding the dog. (Remember, every long journey begins with a single step.) However, on subsequent trials, gradually and progressively increase the length of stay required to receive a reward. In no time at all your dog will stand calmly for a minute or so.

Relevancy Training

Once you have taught the dog what you expect her to do when requested to come, sit, lie down, stand, rollover and stay, the time is right to teach the dog *why* she should comply with your wishes. The secret is to have many (*many*) extremely short training interludes (two to five seconds each) at numerous (*numerous*) times during the course of the dog's day. Especially work with the dog immediately *before* the dog's good times and *during* the dog's good times. For example, ask your dog to sit and/or lie down each time before opening doors, serving meals, offering treats and tummy rubs; ask the dog to perform a few controlled doggy push-ups before letting her off-leash or throwing a tennis ball; and perhaps request the dog to sit-down-sit-stand-down-stand-rollover before inviting her to cuddle on the couch.

Similarly, request the dog to sit many times during play or on walks, and in no time at all the dog will be only too pleased to follow your instructions because he has learned that a compliant response heralds all sorts of goodies. Basically all you are trying to teach the dog is how to say please: "Please throw the tennis ball. Please may I snuggle on the couch."

119

Remember, whereas it is important to keep training interludes short, it is equally important to have many short sessions each and every day. The shortest (and most useful) session comprises asking the dog to sit and then go play during a play session. When trained this way, your dog will soon associate training with good times. In fact, the dog may be unable to distinguish between training and good times and, indeed, there should be no distinction. The warped concept that training involves forcing the dog to comply and/or dominating his will is totally at odds with the picture of a truly well-trained dog. In reality, enjoying a game of training with a dog is no different from enjoying a game of backgammon or tennis with a friend; and walking with a dog should be no different from strolling with buddies on the golf course.

Walk by Your Side

Many people attempt to teach a dog to heel by putting him on a leash and physically correcting the dog when he makes mistakes. There are a number of things seriously wrong with this approach, the first being that most people do not want precision heeling; rather, they simply want the dog to follow or walk by their side. Second, when physically restrained during "training," even though the dog may grudgingly mope by your side when "handcuffed" on leash, let's see what happens when he is off leash. History! The dog is in the next county because he never enjoyed walking with you on leash and you have no control over him off leash. So let's just teach the dog off leash from the outset to *want* to walk with us. Third, if the dog has not been trained to heel, it is a trifle hasty to think about punishing the poor dog for making mistakes and breaking heeling rules he didn't even know existed. This is simply not fair! Surely, if the dog had been adequately taught how to heel, he would seldom make mistakes and hence there would be no need to correct the dog. Remember, each mistake and each correction (punishment) advertise the trainer's inadequacy, not the dog's. The dog is not stubborn, he is not stupid and he is not bad. Even if he were, he would still require training, so let's train him properly.

Let's teach the dog to *enjoy* following us and to *want* to walk by our side offleash. Then it will be easier to teach high-precision off-leash heeling patterns if desired. After attaching the leash for safety on outdoor walks, but before going anywhere, it is necessary to teach the dog specifically not to pull. Now it will be much easier to teach on-leash walking and heeling because the dog already wants to walk with you, he is familiar with the desired walking and heeling positions and he knows not to pull.

FOLLOWING

Start by training your dog to follow you. Many puppies will follow if you simply walk away from them and maybe click your fingers or chuckle. Adult dogs may require additional enticement to stimulate them to follow, such as a training lure or, at the very least, a lively trainer. To teach the dog to follow: (1) keep walking and (2) walk away from the dog. If the dog attempts to lead or lag, change pace; slow down if the dog forges too far ahead, but speed up if he lags too far behind. Say "Steady!" or "Easy!" each time before you slow down and "Quickly!" or "Hustle!" each time before you speed up, and the dog will learn to change pace on cue. If the dog lags or leads too far, or if he wanders right or left, simply walk quickly in the opposite direction and maybe even run away from the dog and hide.

Practicing is a lot of fun; you can set up a course in your home, yard or park to do this. Indoors, entice the dog to follow upstairs, into a bedroom, into the bathroom, downstairs, around the living room couch, zigzagging between dining room chairs and into the kitchen for dinner. Outdoors, get the dog to follow around park benches, trees, shrubs and along walkways and lines in the grass. (For safety outdoors, it is advisable to attach a long line on the dog, but never exert corrective tension on the line.)

Remember, following has a lot to do with attitude—*your* attitude! Most probably your dog will *not* want to follow Mr. Grumpy Troll with the personality of wilted lettuce. Lighten up—walk with a jaunty step, whistle a happy tune, sing, skip and tell jokes to your dog and he will be right there by your side.

BY YOUR SIDE

It is smart to train the dog to walk close on one side or the other—either side will do, your choice. When walking, jogging or cycling, it is generally bad news to have the dog suddenly cut in front of you. In fact, I train my dogs to walk "By my side" and "Other side"—both very useful instructions. It is possible to position the dog fairly accurately by looking to the appropriate side and clicking your fingers or slapping your thigh on that side. A precise positioning may be attained by holding a training lure, such as a chewtoy, tennis ball, or food treat. Stop and stand still several times throughout the walk, just as you would when window shopping or meeting a friend. Use the lure to make sure the dog slows down and stays close whenever you stop.

When teaching the dog to heel, we generally want her to sit in heel position when we stop. Teach heel

Using a toy to teach sit-heel-sit sequences: 1) "Phoenix, heel!" Standing still, move lure up and back over dog's muzzle.... 2) To position dog sitting in heel position on your left side. 3) "Phoenix, heel!" wagging lure in left hand. Change lure to right hand in preparation for sit signal.

position at the standstill and the dog will learn that the default heel position is sitting by your side (left or right—your choice, unless you wish to compete in obedience trials, in which case the dog must heel on the left).

Several times a day, stand up and call your dog to come and sit in heel position—"Fido, heel!" For example, instruct the dog to come to heel each time there are commercials on TV, or each time you turn a page of a novel, and the dog will get it in a single evening.

Practice straight-line heeling and turns separately. With the dog sitting at heel, teach him to turn in place. After each quarter-turn, half-turn or full turn in place, lure the dog to sit at heel. Now it's time for short straight-line heeling sequences, no more than a few steps at a time. Always think of heeling in terms of Sit-Heel-Sit sequences—start and end with the dog in position and do your best to keep him there when moving. Progressively increase the number of steps in each sequence. When the dog remains close for 20 yards of straight-line heeling, it is time to add a few turns and then sign up for a happy-heeling obedience class to get some advice from the experts.

4) Use hand signal only to lure dog to sit as you stop. Eventually, dog will sit automatically at heel whenever you stop. 5) "Good dog!"

NO PULLING ON LEASH

You can start teaching your dog not to pull on leash anywhere—in front of the television or outdoors—but regardless of location, you must not take a single step with tension in the leash. For a reason known only to dogs, even just a couple of paces of pulling on leash is intrinsically motivating and diabolically rewarding. Instead, attach the leash to the dog's collar, grasp the other end firmly with both hands held close to your chest, and stand still—do not budge an inch. Have somebody watch you with a stopwatch to time your progress, or else you will never believe this will work and so you will not even try the exercise, and your shoulder and the dog's neck will be traumatized for years to come.

Stand still and wait for the dog to stop pulling, and to sit and/or lie down. All dogs stop pulling and sit eventually. Most take only a couple of minutes; the all-time record is 22 ⅕ minutes. Time how long it takes. Gently praise the dog when he stops pulling, and as soon as he sits, enthusiastically praise the dog and take just one step forwards, then immediately stand still. This single step usually demonstrates the ballistic reinforcing nature of pulling on leash; most dogs explode to the end of the leash, so be prepared for the strain. Stand firm and wait for the dog to sit again. Repeat this half a dozen times and you will probably notice a progressive reduction in the force of the dog's one-step explosions and a radical reduction in the time it takes for the dog to sit each time.

As the dog learns "Sit we go" and "Pull we stop," she will begin to walk forward calmly with each single step and automatically sit when you stop. Now try two steps before you stop. Wooooooo! Scary! When the dog has mastered two steps at a time, try for three. After each success, progressively increase the number of steps in the sequence: try four steps and then six, eight, ten and twenty steps before stopping. Congratulations! You are now walking the dog on leash.

Whenever walking with the dog (off leash or on leash), make sure you stop periodically to practice a few position commands and stays before instructing the dog to "Walk on!" (Remember, you want the dog to be compliant everywhere, not just in the kitchen when his dinner is at hand.) For example, stopping every 25 yards to briefly train the dog amounts to over 200 training interludes within a single three-mile stroll. And each training session is in a different location. You will not believe the improvement within just the first mile of the first walk.

To put it another way, integrating training into a walk offers 200 separate opportunities to use the continuance of the walk as a reward to reinforce the dog's education. Moreover, some training interludes may comprise continuing education for the dog's walking skills: Alternate short periods of the dog walking calmly by your side with periods when the dog is allowed to sniff and investigate the environment. Now sniffing odors on the grass and meeting other dogs become rewards which reinforce the dog's calm and mannerly demeanor. Good Lord! Whatever next? Many enjoyable walks together of course. Happy trails!

THE IMPORTANCE OF TRICKS

Nothing will improve a dog's quality of life better than having a few tricks under its belt. Teaching any trick expands the dog's vocabulary, which facilitates communication and improves the owner's control. Also, specific tricks help prevent and resolve specific behavior problems. For example, by teaching the dog to fetch his toys, the dog learns carrying a toy makes the owner happy and, therefore, will be more likely to chew his toy than other inappropriate items.

More important, teaching tricks prompts owners to lighten up and train with a sunny disposition. Really, tricks should be no different from any other behaviors we put on cue. But they are. When teaching tricks, owners have a much sweeter attitude, which in turn motivates the dog and improves her willingness to comply. The dog feels tricks are a blast, but formal commands are a drag. In fact, tricks are so enjoyable, they may be used as rewards in training by asking the dog to come, sit and down-stay and then rollover for a tummy rub. Go on, try it: Crack a smile and even giggle when the dog promptly and willingly lies down and stays.

Most important, performing tricks prompts onlookers to smile and giggle. Many people are scared of dogs, especially large ones. And nothing can be more off-putting for a dog than to be constantly confronted by strangers who don't like him because of his size or the way he looks. Uneasy people put the dog on edge, causing him to back off and bark, only frightening people all the more. And so a vicious circle develops, with the people's fear fueling the dog's fear *and vice versa*. Instead, tie a pink ribbon to your dog's collar and practice all sorts of tricks on walks and in the park, and you will be pleasantly amazed how it changes people's attitudes toward your friendly dog. The dog's repertoire of tricks is limited only by the trainer's imagination. Below I have described three of my favorites:

SPEAK AND SHUSH

The training sequence involved in teaching a dog to bark on request is no different from that used when training any behavior on cue: request—lure—response—reward. As always, the secret of success lies in finding an effective lure. If the dog always barks at the doorbell, for example, say "Rover, speak!", have an accomplice ring the doorbell, then reward the dog for barking. After a few woofs, ask Rover to "Shush!", waggle a food treat under his nose (to entice him to sniff and thus to shush), praise him when quiet and eventually offer the treat as a reward. Alternate "Speak" and "Shush," progressively increasing the length of shush-time between each barking bout.

PLAYBOW

With the dog standing, say "Bow!" and lower the food lure (palm upwards) to rest between the dog's forepaws. Praise as the dog lowers

her forequarters and sternum to the ground (as when teaching the down), but then lure the dog to stand and offer the treat. On successive trials, gradually increase the length of time the dog is required to remain in the playbow posture in order to gain a food reward. If the dog's rear end collapses into a down, say nothing and offer no reward; simply start over.

BE A BEAR

With the dog sitting backed into a corner to prevent him from toppling over backwards, say "Be a Bear!" With bent paw and palm down, raise a lure upwards and backwards along the top of the dog's muzzle. Praise the dog when he sits up on his haunches and offer the treat as a reward. To prevent the dog from standing on his hind legs, keep the lure closer to the dog's muzzle. On each trial, progressively increase the length of time the dog is required to sit up to receive a food reward. Since lure/reward training is so easy, teach the dog to stand and walk on his hind legs as well!

Teaching "Be a Bear"

chapter 9

Getting
Active
with your Dog

by Bardi McLennan

Once you and your dog have graduated from basic obedience training and are beginning to work together as a team, you can take part in the growing world of dog activities. There are so many fun things to do with your dog! Just remember, people and dogs don't always learn at the same pace, so don't be upset if you (or your dog) need more than two basic training courses before your team becomes operational. Even smart dogs don't go straight to college from kindergarten!

Just as there are events geared to certain types of dogs, so there are ones that are more appealing to certain types of people. In some activities, you give the commands and your dog does the work (upland game hunting is one example), while in others, such as agility, you'll both get a workout. You may want to aim for prestigious titles to add to your dog's name, or you may want nothing more than the sheer enjoyment of being around other people and their dogs. Passive or active, participation has its own rewards.

Consider your dog's physical capabilities when looking into any of the canine activities. It's easy to see that a Basset Hound is not built for the racetrack, nor would a Chihuahua be the breed of choice for pulling a sled. A loyal dog will attempt almost anything you ask him to do, so it is up to you to know your dog's limitations. A dog must be physically sound in order to compete at any level in athletic activities, and being mentally sound is a definite plus. Advanced age, however, may not be a deterrent. Many dogs still hunt and herd at ten or twelve years of age. It's entirely possible for dogs to be "fit at 50." Take your dog for a checkup, explain to your vet the type of activity you have in mind and be guided by his or her findings.

All dogs seem to love playing flyball.

You needn't be restricted to breed-specific sports if it's only fun you're after. Certain AKC activities are limited to designated breeds; however, as each new trial, test or sport has grown in popularity, so has the variety of breeds encouraged to participate at a fun level.

But don't shortchange your fun, or that of your dog, by thinking only of the basic function of her breed. Once a dog has learned how to learn, she can be taught to do just about anything as long as the size of the dog is right for the job and you both think it is fun and rewarding. In other words, you are a team.

To get involved in any of the activities detailed in this chapter, look for the names and addresses of the organizations that sponsor them in Chapter 13. You can also ask your breeder or a local dog trainer for contacts.

You can compete in obedience trials with a well trained dog.

Official American Kennel Club Activities

The following tests and trials are some of the events sanctioned by the AKC and sponsored by various dog clubs. Your dog's expertise will be rewarded with impressive titles. You can participate just for fun, or be competitive and go for those awards.

OBEDIENCE

Training classes begin with pups as young as three months of age in kindergarten puppy training, then advance to pre-novice (all exercises on lead) and go on to novice, which is where you'll start off-lead work. In obedience classes dogs learn to sit, stay, heel and come through a variety of exercises. Once you've got the basics down, you can enter obedience trials and work toward earning your dog's first degree, a C.D. (Companion Dog).

The next level is called "Open," in which jumps and retrieves perk up the dog's interest. Passing grades in competition at this level earn a C.D.X. (Companion Dog Excellent). Beyond that lies the goal of the most ambitious—Utility (U.D. and even U.D.X. or OTCh, an Obedience Champion).

AGILITY

All dogs can participate in the latest canine sport to have gained worldwide popularity for its fun and excitement, agility. It began in England as a canine version of horse show-jumping, but because dogs are more agile and able to perform on verbal commands, extra feats were added such as climbing, balancing and racing through tunnels or in and out of weave poles. Many of the obstacles (regulation or homemade) can be set up in your own backyard. If the agility bug bites, you could end up in international competition!

For starters, your dog should be obedience trained, even though, in the beginning, the lessons may all be taught on lead. Once the dog understands the commands (and you do, too), it's as easy as guiding the dog over a prescribed course, one obstacle at a time. In competition, the race is against the clock, so wear your running shoes! The dog starts with 200 points and the judge deducts for infractions and misadventures along the way.

All dogs seem to love agility and respond to it as if they were being turned loose in a playground paradise. Your dog's enthusiasm will be contagious; agility turns into great fun for dog and owner.

FIELD TRIALS AND HUNTING TESTS

There are field trials and hunting tests for the sporting breeds—retrievers, spaniels and pointing breeds, and for some hounds—Bassets, Beagles and Dachshunds. Field trials are competitive events that test a dog's ability to perform the functions for which she was bred. Hunting tests, which are open to retrievers,

---

TITLES AWARDED BY THE AKC

Conformation: Ch. (Champion)

Obedience: CD (Companion Dog); CDX (Companion Dog Excellent); UD (Utility Dog); UDX (Utility Dog Excellent); OTCh. (Obedience Trial Champion)

Field: JH (Junior Hunter); SH (Senior Hunter); MH (Master Hunter); AFCh. (Amateur Field Champion); FCh. (Field Champion)

Lure Coursing: JC (Junior Courser); SC (Senior Courser)

Herding: HT (Herding Tested); PT (Pre-Trial Tested); HS (Herding Started); HI (Herding Intermediate); HX (Herding Excellent); HCh. (Herding Champion)

Tracking: TD (Tracking Dog); TDX (Tracking Dog Excellent)

Agility: NAD (Novice Agility); OAD (Open Agility); ADX (Agility Excellent); MAX (Master Agility)

Earthdog Tests: JE (Junior Earthdog); SE (Senior Earthdog); ME (Master Earthdog)

Canine Good Citizen: CGC

Combination: DC (Dual Champion—Ch. and Fch.); TC (Triple Champion—Ch., Fch., and OTCh.)

spaniels and pointing breeds only, are noncompetitive and are a means of judging the dog's ability as well as that of the handler.

Hunting is a very large and complex part of canine sports, and if you own one of the breeds that hunts, the events are a great treat for your dog and you. He gets to do what he was bred for, and you get to work with him and watch him do it. You'll be proud of and amazed at what your dog can do.

Fortunately, the AKC publishes a series of booklets on these events, which outline the rules and regulations and include a glossary of the sometimes complicated terms. The AKC also publishes newsletters for field trialers and hunting test enthusiasts. The United Kennel Club (UKC) also has informative materials for the hunter and his dog.

Retrievers and other sporting breeds get to do what they're bred to in hunting tests.

HERDING TESTS AND TRIALS

Herding, like hunting, dates back to the first known uses man made of dogs. The interest in herding today is widespread, and if you own a herding breed, you can join in the activity. Herding dogs are tested for their natural skills to keep a flock of ducks, sheep or cattle together. If your dog shows potential, you can start at the testing level, where your dog can earn a title for showing an inherent herding ability. With training you can advance to the trial level, where your dog should be capable of controlling even difficult livestock in diverse situations.

LURE COURSING

The AKC Tests and Trials for Lure Coursing are open to traditional sighthounds—Greyhounds, Whippets,

Borzoi, Salukis, Afghan Hounds, Ibizan Hounds and Scottish Deerhounds—as well as to Basenjis and Rhodesian Ridgebacks. Hounds are judged on overall ability, follow, speed, agility and endurance. This is possibly the most exciting of the trials for spectators, because the speed and agility of the dogs is awesome to watch as they chase the lure (or "course") in heats of two or three dogs at a time.

TRACKING

Tracking is another activity in which almost any dog can compete because every dog that sniffs the ground when taken outdoors is, in fact, tracking. The hard part comes when the rules as to what, when and where the dog tracks are determined by a person, not the dog! Tracking tests cover a large area of fields, woods and roads. The tracks are laid hours before the dogs go to work on them, and include "tricks" like cross-tracks and sharp turns. If you're interested in search-and-rescue work, this is the place to start.

This tracking dog is hot on the trail.

EARTHDOG TESTS FOR SMALL TERRIERS AND DACHSHUNDS

These tests are open to Australian, Bedlington, Border, Cairn, Dandie Dinmont, Smooth and Wire Fox, Lakeland, Norfolk, Norwich, Scottish, Sealyham, Skye, Welsh and West Highland White Terriers as well as Dachshunds. The dogs need no prior training for this terrier sport. There is a qualifying test on the day of the event, so dog and handler learn the rules on the spot. These tests, or "digs," sometimes end with informal races in the late afternoon.

Here are some of the extracurricular obedience and racing activities that are not regulated by the AKC or UKC, but are generally run by clubs or a group of dog fanciers and are often open to all.

Canine Freestyle This activity is something new on the scene and is variously likened to dancing, dressage or ice skating. It is meant to show the athleticism of the dog, but also requires showmanship on the part of the dog's handler. If you and your dog like to ham it up for friends, you might want to look into freestyle.

Lure coursing lets sighthounds do what they do best—run!

Scent Hurdle Racing Scent hurdle racing is purely a fun activity sponsored by obedience clubs with members forming competing teams. The height of the hurdles is based on the size of the shortest dog on the team. On a signal, one team dog is released on each of two side-by-side courses and must clear every hurdle before picking up its own dumbbell from a platform and returning over the jumps to the handler. As each dog returns, the next on that team is sent. Of course, that is what the dogs are supposed to do. When the dogs improvise (going under or around the hurdles, stealing another dog's dumbbell, and so forth), it no doubt frustrates the handlers, but just adds to the fun for everyone else.

Flyball This type of racing is similar, but after negotiating the four hurdles, the dog comes to a flyball box, steps on a lever that releases a tennis ball into the air, catches the ball and returns over the hurdles to the starting point. This game also becomes extremely fun for spectators because the dogs sometimes cheat by catching a ball released by the dog in the next lane. Three titles can be earned—Flyball Dog (F.D.), Flyball Dog Excellent (F.D.X.) and Flyball Dog Champion (Fb.D.Ch.)—all awarded by the North American Flyball Association, Inc.

Dogsledding The name conjures up the Rocky Mountains or the frigid North, but you can find dogsled clubs in such unlikely spots as Maryland, North Carolina and Virginia! Dogsledding is primarily for the Nordic breeds such as the Alaskan Malamutes, Siberian Huskies and Samoyeds, but other breeds can try. There are some practical backyard applications to this sport, too. With parental supervision, almost any strong dog could pull a child's sled.

Coming over the A-frame on an agility course.

These are just some of the many recreational ways you can get to know and understand your multifaceted dog better and have fun doing it.

Your Dog
and your
Family

by Bardi McLennan

Adding a dog automatically increases your family by one, no matter whether you live alone in an apartment or are part of a mother, father and six kids household. The single-person family is fair game for numerous and varied canine misconceptions as to who is dog and who pays the bills, whereas a dog in a houseful of children will consider himself to be just one of the gang, littermates all. One dog and one child may give a dog reason to believe they are both kids or both dogs. Either interpretation requires parental supervision and sometimes speedy intervention.

As soon as one paw goes through the door into your home, Rufus (or Rufina) has to make many adjustments to become a part of your

136

family. Your job is to make him fit in as painlessly as possible. An older dog may have some frame of reference from past experience, but to a 10-week-old puppy, everything is brand new: people, furniture, stairs, when and where people eat, sleep or watch TV, his own place and everyone else's space, smells, sounds, outdoors—everything!

Puppies, and newly acquired dogs of any age, do not need what we think of as "freedom." If you leave a new dog or puppy loose in the house, you will almost certainly return to chaotic destruction and the dog will forever after equate your homecoming with a time of punishment to be dreaded. It is unfair to give your dog what amounts to "freedom to get into trouble." Instead, confine him to a crate for brief periods of your absence (up to three or four hours) and, for the long haul, a workday for example, confine him to one untrashable area with his own toys, a bowl of water and a radio left on (low) in another room.

Lots of pets get along with each other just fine.

For the first few days, when not confined, put Rufus on a long leash tied to your wrist or waist. This umbilical cord method enables the dog to learn all about you from your body language and voice, and to learn by his own actions which things in the house are NO! and which ones are rewarded by "Good dog." Housetraining will be easier with the pup always by your side. Speaking of which, accidents do happen. That goal of "completely housetrained" takes up to a year, or the length of time it takes the pup to mature.

The All-Adult Family

Most dogs in an adults-only household today are likely to be latchkey pets, with no one home all day but the dog. When you return after a tough day on the job, the dog can and should be your relaxation therapy. But going home can instead be a daily frustration.

Separation anxiety is a very common problem for the dog in a working household. It may begin with whines and barks of loneliness, but it will soon escalate into a frenzied destruction derby. That is why it is so important to set aside the time to teach a dog to relax when left alone in his confined area and to understand that he can trust you to return.

Let the dog get used to your work schedule in easy stages. Confine him to one room and go in and out of that room over and over again. Be casual about it. No physical, voice or eye contact. When the pup no longer even notices your comings and goings, leave the house for varying lengths of time, returning to stay home for a few minutes and gradually increasing the time away. This training can take days, but the dog is learning that you haven't left him forever and that he can trust you.

Any time you leave the dog, but especially during this training period, be casual about your departure. No anxiety-building fond farewells. Just "Bye" and go! Remember the "Good dog" when you return to find everything more or less as you left it.

If things are a mess (or even a disaster) when you return, greet the dog, take him outside to eliminate, and then put him in his crate while you clean up. Rant and rave in the shower! *Do not* punish the dog. You were not there when it happened, and the rule is: Only punish as you catch the dog in the act of wrongdoing. Obviously, it makes sense to get your latchkey puppy when you'll have a week or two to spend on these training essentials.

Family weekend activities should include Rufus whenever possible. Depending on the pup's age, now is the time for a long walk in the park, playtime in the backyard, a hike in the woods. Socializing is as important as health care, good food and physical exercise, so visiting Aunt Emma or Uncle Harry and the next-door neighbor's dog or cat is essential to developing an outgoing, friendly temperament in your pet.

If you are a single adult, socializing Rufus at home and away will prevent him from becoming overly protective of you (or just overly attached) and will also prevent such behavioral problems as dominance or fear of strangers.

Babies

Whether already here or on the way, babies figure larger than life in the eyes of a dog. If the dog is there first, let him in on all your baby preparations in the house. When baby arrives, let Rufus sniff any item of clothing that has been on the baby before Junior comes home. Then let Mom greet the dog first before introducing the new family member. Hold the baby down for the dog to see and sniff, but make sure someone's holding the dog on lead in case of any sudden moves. Don't play keep-away or tease the dog with the baby, which only invites undesirable jumping up.

The dog and the baby are "family," and for starters can be treated almost as equals. Things rapidly change, however, especially when baby takes to creeping around on all fours on the dog's turf or, better yet, has yummy pudding all over her face and hands! That's when a lot of things in the dog's and baby's lives become more separate than equal.

Dogs are perfect confidants.

Toddlers make terrible dog owners, but if you can't avoid the combination, use patient discipline (that is, positive teaching rather than punishment), and use time-outs before you run out of patience.

A dog and a baby (or toddler, or an assertive young child) should never be left alone together. Take the dog with you or confine him. With a baby or youngsters in the house, you'll have plenty of use for that wonderful canine safety device called a crate!

Young Children

Any dog in a house with kids will behave pretty much as the kids do, good or bad. But even good dogs and good children can get into trouble when play becomes rowdy and active.

Legs bobbing up and down, shrill voices screeching, a ball hurtling overhead, all add up to exuberant frustration for a dog who's just trying to be part of the gang. In a pack of puppies, any legs or toys being chased would be caught by a set of teeth, and all the pups involved would understand that is how the game is played. Kids do not understand this, nor do parents tolerate it. Bring Rufus indoors before you have reason to regret it. This is time-out, not a punishment.

Teach children how to play nicely with a puppy.

You can explain the situation to the children and tell them they must play quieter games until the puppy learns not to grab them with his mouth. Unfortunately, you can't explain it that easily to the dog. With adult supervision, they will learn how to play together.

Young children love to tease. Sticking their faces or wiggling their hands or fingers in the dog's face is teasing. To another person it might be just annoying, but it is threatening to a dog. There's another difference: We can make the child stop by an explanation, but the only way a dog can stop it is with a warning growl and then with teeth. Teasing is the major cause of children being bitten by their pets. Treat it seriously.

Older Children

The best age for a child to get a first dog is between the ages of 8 and 12. That's when kids are able to accept some real responsibility for their pet. Even so, take the child's vow of "I will never *ever* forget to feed (brush, walk, etc.) the dog" for what it's worth: a child's good intention at that moment. Most kids today have extra lessons, soccer practice, Little League, ballet, and so forth piled on top of school schedules. There will be many times when Mom will have to come to the dog's rescue. "I walked the dog for you so you can set the table for me" is one way to get around a missed appointment without laying on blame or guilt.

Kids in this age group make excellent obedience trainers because they are into the teaching/learning process themselves and they lack the self-consciousness of adults. Attending a dog show is something the whole family can enjoy, and watching Junior Showmanship may catch the eye of the kids. Older children can begin to get involved in many of the recreational activities that were reviewed in the previous chapter. Some of the agility obstacles, for example, can be set up in the backyard as a family project (with an adult making sure all the equipment is safe and secure for the dog).

Older kids are also beginning to look to the future, and may envision themselves as veterinarians or trainers or show dog handlers or writers of the next Lassie best-seller. Dogs are perfect confidants for these dreams. They won't tell a soul.

Other Pets

Introduce all pets tactfully. In a dog/cat situation, hold the dog, not the cat. Let two dogs meet on neutral turf—a stroll in the park or a walk down the street—with both on loose leads to permit all the normal canine ways of saying hello, including routine sniffing, circling, more sniffing, and so on. Small creatures such as hamsters, chinchillas or mice must be kept safe from their natural predators (dogs and cats).

Festive Family Occasions

Parties are great for people, but not necessarily for puppies. Until all the guests have arrived, put the dog in his crate or in a room where he won't be disturbed. A socialized dog can join the fun later as long as he's not underfoot, annoying guests or into the hors d'oeuvres.

There are a few dangers to consider, too. Doors opening and closing can allow a puppy to slip out unnoticed in the confusion, and you'll be organizing a search party instead of playing host or hostess. Party food and buffet service are not for dogs. Let Rufus party in his crate with a nice big dog biscuit.

At Christmas time, not only are tree decorations dangerous and breakable (and perhaps family heirlooms), but extreme caution should be taken with the lights, cords and outlets for the tree lights and any other festive lighting. Occasionally a dog lifts a leg, ignoring the fact that the tree is indoors. To avoid this, use a canine repellent, made for gardens, on the tree. Or keep him out of the tree room unless supervised. And whatever you do, *don't* invite trouble by hanging his toys on the tree!

Car Travel

Before you plan a vacation by car or RV with Rufus, be sure he enjoys car travel. Nothing spoils a holiday quicker than a carsick dog! Work within the dog's comfort level. Get in the car with the dog in his crate or attached to a canine car safety belt and just sit there until he relaxes. That's all. Next time, get in the car, turn on the engine and go nowhere. Just sit. When that is okay, turn on the engine and go around the block. Now you can go for a ride and include a stop where you get out, leaving the dog for a minute or two.

On a warm day, always park in the shade and leave windows open several inches. And return quickly. It only takes 10 minutes for a car to become an overheated steel death trap.

Motel or Pet Motel?

Not all motels or hotels accept pets, but you have a much better choice today than even a few years ago. To find a dog-friendly lodging, look at *On the Road Again With Man's Best Friend*, a series of directories that detail bed and breakfasts, inns, family resorts and other hotels/motels. Some places require a refundable deposit to cover any damage incurred by the dog. More B&Bs accept pets now, but some restrict the size.

If taking Rufus with you is not feasible, check out boarding kennels in your area. Your veterinarian may offer this service, or recommend a kennel or two he or she is familiar with. Go see the facilities for yourself, ask about exercise, diet, housing, and so on. Or, if you'd rather have Rufus stay home, look into bonded petsitters, many of whom will also bring in the mail and water your plants.

11

Your Dog
and your
Community

by Bardi McLennan

Step outside your home with your dog and you are no longer just family, you are both part of your community. This is when the phrase "responsible pet ownership" takes on serious implications. For starters, it means you pick up after your dog—not just occasionally, but every time your dog eliminates away from home. That means you have joined the Plastic Baggy Brigade! You always have plastic sandwich bags in your pocket and several in the car. It means you teach your kids how to use them, too. If you think this is "yucky," just imagine what

the person (a non-doggy person) who inadvertently steps in the mess thinks!

Your responsibility extends to your neighbors: To their ears (no annoying barking); to their property (their garbage, their lawn, their flower beds, their cat— especially their cat); to their kids (on bikes, at play); to their kids' toys and sports equipment.

There are numerous dog-related laws, ranging from simple dog licensing and leash laws to those holding you liable for any physical injury or property damage done by your dog. These laws are in place to protect everyone in the community, including you and your dog. There are town ordinances and state laws which are by no means the same in all towns or all states. Ignorance of the law won't get you off the hook. The time to find out what the laws are where you live is now.

Be sure your dog's license is current. This is not just a good local ordinance, it can make the difference between finding your lost dog or not. Many states now require proof of rabies vaccination and that the dog has been spayed or neutered before issuing a license. At the same time, keep up the dog's annual immunizations.

Dressing your dog up makes him appealing to strangers.

Never let your dog run loose in the neighborhood. This will not only keep you on the right side of the leash law, it's the outdoor version of the rule about not giving your dog "freedom to get into trouble."

Good Canine Citizen

Sometimes it's hard for a dog's owner to assess whether or not the dog is sufficiently socialized to be accepted by the community at large. Does Rufus or Rufina display good, controlled behavior in public? The AKC's Canine Good Citizen program is available through many dog organizations. If your dog passes the test, the title "CGC" is earned.

The overall purpose is to turn your dog into a good neighbor and to teach you about your responsibility to your community as a dog owner. Here are the ten things your dog must do willingly:

1. Accept a stranger stopping to chat with you.
2. Sit and be petted by a stranger.
3. Allow a stranger to handle him or her as a groomer or veterinarian would.
4. Walk nicely on a loose lead.
5. Walk calmly through a crowd.
6. Sit and down on command, then stay in a sit or down position while you walk away.
7. Come when called.
8. Casually greet another dog.
9. React confidently to distractions.
10. Accept being left alone with someone other than you and not become overly agitated or nervous.

Schools and Dogs

Schools are getting involved with pet ownership on an educational level. It has been proven that children who are kind to animals are humane in their attitude toward other people as adults.

A dog is a child's best friend, and so children are often primary pet owners, if not the primary caregivers. Unfortunately, they are also the ones most often bitten by dogs. This occurs due to a lack of understanding that pets, no matter how sweet, cuddly and loving, are still animals. Schools, along with parents, dog clubs, dog fanciers and the AKC, are working to change all that with video programs for children not only in grade school, but in the nursery school and pre-kindergarten age group. Teaching youngsters how to be responsible dog owners is important community work. When your dog has a CGC, volunteer to take part in an educational classroom event put on by your dog club.

Boy Scout Merit Badge

A Merit Badge for Dog Care can be earned by any Boy Scout ages 11 to 18. The requirements are not easy, but amount to a complete course in responsible dog care and general ownership. Here are just a few of the things a Scout must do to earn that badge:

Point out ten parts of the dog using the correct names.

Give a report (signed by parent or guardian) on your care of the dog (feeding, food used, housing, exercising, grooming and bathing), plus what has been done to keep the dog healthy.

Explain the right way to obedience train a dog, and demonstrate three comments.

Several of the requirements have to do with health care, including first aid, handling a hurt dog, and the dangers of home treatment for a serious ailment.

The final requirement is to know the local laws and ordinances involving dogs.

There are similar programs for Girl Scouts and 4-H members.

Local Clubs

Local dog clubs are no longer in existence just to put on a yearly dog show. Today, they are apt to be the hub of the community's involvement with pets. Dog clubs conduct educational forums with big-name speakers, stage demonstrations of canine talent in a busy mall and take dogs of various breeds to schools for class-room discussion.

The quickest way to feel accepted as a member in a club is to volunteer your services! Offer to help with something—anything—and watch your popularity (and your interest) grow.

Therapy Dogs

Once your dog has earned that essential CGC and reliably demonstrates a steady, calm temperament, you could look into what therapy dogs are doing in your area.

Therapy dogs go with their owners to visit patients at hospitals or nursing homes, generally remaining on leash but able to coax a pat from a stiffened hand, a smile from a blank face, a few words from sealed lips or a hug from someone in need of love.

Nursing homes cover a wide range of patient care. Some specialize in care of the elderly, some in the treatment of specific illnesses, some in physical therapy. Children's facilities also welcome visits from trained therapy dogs for boosting morale in their pediatric patients. Hospice care for the terminally ill and the at-home care of AIDS patients are other areas where this canine visiting is desperately needed. Therapy dog training comes first.

Your dog can make a difference in lots of lives.

There is a lot more involved than just taking your nice friendly pooch to someone's bedside. Doing therapy dog work involves your own emotional stability as well as that of your dog. But once you have met all the requirements for this work, making the rounds once a week or once a month with your therapy dog is possibly the most rewarding of all community activities.

Disaster Aid

This community service is definitely not for everyone, partly because it is time-consuming. The initial training is rigorous, and there can be no let-up in the continuing workouts, because members are on call 24 hours a day to go wherever they are needed at a moment's notice. But if you think you would like to be able to assist in a disaster, look into search-and-rescue work. The network of search-and-rescue volunteers is worldwide, and all members of the American Rescue Dog Association (ARDA) who are qualified to do this work are volunteers who train and maintain their own dogs.

Physical Aid

Most people are familiar with Seeing Eye dogs, which serve as blind people's eyes, but not with all the other work that dogs are trained to do to assist the disabled. Dogs are also specially trained to pull wheelchairs, carry school books, pick up dropped objects, open and close doors. Some also are ears for the deaf. All these assistance-trained dogs, by the way, are allowed anywhere "No Pet" signs exist (as are therapy dogs when

Making the rounds with your therapy dog can be very rewarding.

properly identified). Getting started in any of this fascinating work requires a background in dog training and canine behavior, but there are also volunteer jobs ranging from answering the phone to cleaning out kennels to providing a foster home for a puppy. You have only to ask.

part four

Beyond
the
Basics

chapter 12

Recommended Reading

Books

ABOUT HEALTH CARE

Ackerman, Lowell. *Guide to Skin and Haircoat Problems in Dogs.* Loveland, Colo.: Alpine Publications, 1994.

Alderton, David. *The Dog Care Manual.* Hauppauge, N.Y.: Barron's Educational Series, Inc., 1986.

American Kennel Club. *American Kennel Club Dog Care and Training.* New York: Howell Book House, 1991.

Bamberger, Michelle, DVM. *Help! The Quick Guide to First Aid for Your Dog.* New York: Howell Book House, 1995.

Carlson, Delbert, DVM, and James Giffin, MD. *Dog Owner's Home Veterinary Handbook.* New York: Howell Book House, 1992.

DeBitetto, James, DVM, and Sarah Hodgson. *You & Your Puppy.* New York: Howell Book House, 1995.

Humphries, Jim, DVM. *Dr. Jim's Animal Clinic for Dogs.* New York: Howell Book House, 1994.

McGinnis, Terri. *The Well Dog Book.* New York: Random House, 1991.

Pitcairn, Richard and Susan. *Natural Health for Dogs.* Emmaus, Pa.: Rodale Press, 1982.

ABOUT DOG SHOWS

Hall, Lynn. *Dog Showing for Beginners.* New York: Howell Book House, 1994.

Nichols, Virginia Tuck. *How to Show Your Own Dog.* Neptune, N. J.: TFH, 1970.

Vanacore, Connie. *Dog Showing, An Owner's Guide.* New York: Howell Book House, 1990.

ABOUT TRAINING

Ammen, Amy. *Training in No Time*. New York: Howell Book House, 1995.

Baer, Ted. *Communicating With Your Dog*. Hauppauge, N.Y.: Barron's Educational Series, Inc., 1989.

Benjamin, Carol Lea. *Dog Problems*. New York: Howell Book House, 1989.

Benjamin, Carol Lea. *Dog Training for Kids*. New York: Howell Book House, 1988.

Benjamin, Carol Lea. *Mother Knows Best*. New York: Howell Book House, 1985.

Benjamin, Carol Lea. *Surviving Your Dog's Adolescence*. New York: Howell Book House, 1993.

Bohnenkamp, Gwen. *Manners for the Modern Dog*. San Francisco: Perfect Paws, 1990.

Dibra, Bashkim. *Dog Training by Bash*. New York: Dell, 1992.

Dunbar, Ian, PhD, MRCVS. *Dr. Dunbar's Good Little Dog Book*, James & Kenneth Publishers, 2140 Shattuck Ave. #2406, Berkeley, Calif. 94704. (510) 658–8588. Order from the publisher.

Dunbar, Ian, PhD, MRCVS. *How to Teach a New Dog Old Tricks*, James & Kenneth Publishers. Order from the publisher; address above.

Dunbar, Ian, PhD, MRCVS, and Gwen Bohnenkamp. Booklets on *Preventing Aggression; Housetraining; Chewing; Digging; Barking; Socialization; Fearfulness; and Fighting*, James & Kenneth Publishers. Order from the publisher; address above.

Evans, Job Michael. *People, Pooches and Problems*. New York: Howell Book House, 1991.

Kilcommons, Brian and Sarah Wilson. *Good Owners, Great Dogs*. New York: Warner Books, 1992.

McMains, Joel M. *Dog Logic—Companion Obedience*. New York: Howell Book House, 1992.

Rutherford, Clarice and David H. Neil, MRCVS. *How to Raise a Puppy You Can Live With*. Loveland, Colo.: Alpine Publications, 1982.

Volhard, Jack and Melissa Bartlett. *What All Good Dogs Should Know: The Sensible Way to Train*. New York: Howell Book House, 1991.

ABOUT BREEDING

Harris, Beth J. Finder. *Breeding a Litter, The Complete Book of Prenatal and Postnatal Care*. New York: Howell Book House, 1983.

Holst, Phyllis, DVM. *Canine Reproduction*. Loveland, Colo.: Alpine Publications, 1985.

Walkowicz, Chris and Bonnie Wilcox, DVM. *Successful Dog Breeding, The Complete Handbook of Canine Midwifery*. New York: Howell Book House, 1994.

ABOUT ACTIVITIES

American Rescue Dog Association. *Search and Rescue Dogs*. New York: Howell Book House, 1991.

Barwig, Susan and Stewart Hilliard. *Schutzhund*. New York: Howell Book House, 1991.

Beaman, Arthur S. *Lure Coursing*. New York: Howell Book House, 1994.

Daniels, Julie. *Enjoying Dog Agility—From Backyard to Competition*. New York: Doral Publishing, 1990.

Davis, Kathy Diamond. *Therapy Dogs*. New York: Howell Book House, 1992.

Gallup, Davis Anne. *Running With Man's Best Friend*. Loveland, Colo.: Alpine Publications, 1986.

Habgood, Dawn and Robert. *On the Road Again With Man's Best Friend*. New England, Mid-Atlantic, West Coast and Southeast editions. Selective guides to area bed and breakfasts, inns, hotels and resorts that welcome guests and their dogs. New York: Howell Book House, 1995.

Holland, Vergil S. *Herding Dogs*. New York: Howell Book House, 1994.

LaBelle, Charlene G. *Backpacking With Your Dog*. Loveland, Colo.: Alpine Publications, 1993.

Simmons-Moake, Jane. *Agility Training, The Fun Sport for All Dogs*. New York: Howell Book House, 1991.

Spencer, James B. *Hup! Training Flushing Spaniels the American Way*. New York: Howell Book House, 1992.

Spencer, James B. *Point! Training the All-Seasons Birddog*. New York: Howell Book House, 1995.

Tarrant, Bill. *Training the Hunting Retriever*. New York: Howell Book House, 1991.

Volhard, Jack and Wendy. *The Canine Good Citizen*. New York: Howell Book House, 1994.

General Titles

Haggerty, Captain Arthur J. *How to Get Your Pet Into Show Business*. New York: Howell Book House, 1994.

McLennan, Bardi. *Dogs and Kids, Parenting Tips*. New York: Howell Book House, 1993.

Moran, Patti J. *Pet Sitting for Profit, A Complete Manual for Professional Success*. New York: Howell Book House, 1992.

Scalisi, Danny and Libby Moses. *When Rover Just Won't Do, Over 2,000 Suggestions for Naming Your Dog.* New York: Howell Book House, 1993.

Sife, Wallace, PhD. *The Loss of a Pet.* New York: Howell Book House, 1993.

Wrede, Barbara J. *Civilizing Your Puppy.* Hauppauge, N.Y.: Barron's Educational Series, 1992.

Magazines

The AKC GAZETTE, The Official Journal for the Sport of Purebred Dogs. American Kennel Club, 51 Madison Ave., New York, NY.

Bloodlines Journal. United Kennel Club, 100 E. Kilgore Rd., Kalamazoo, MI.

Dog Fancy. Fancy Publications, 3 Burroughs, Irvine, CA 92718

Dog World. Maclean Hunter Publishing Corp., 29 N. Wacker Dr., Chicago, IL 60606.

Videos

"SIRIUS Puppy Training," by Ian Dunbar, PhD, MRCVS. James & Kenneth Publishers, 2140 Shattuck Ave. #2406, Berkeley, CA 94704. Order from the publisher.

"Training the Companion Dog," from Dr. Dunbar's British TV Series, James & Kenneth Publishers. (See address above).

The American Kennel Club produces videos on every breed of dog, as well as on hunting tests, field trials and other areas of interest to purebred dog owners. For more information, write to AKC/Video Fulfillment, 5580 Centerview Dr., Suite 200, Raleigh, NC 27606.

Resources

Breed Clubs

Every breed recognized by the American Kennel Club has a national (parent) club. National clubs are a great source of information on your breed. You can get the name of the secretary of the club by contacting:

The American Kennel Club
51 Madison Avenue
New York, NY 10010
(212) 696-8200

There are also numerous all-breed, individual breed, obedience, hunting and other special-interest dog clubs across the country. The American Kennel Club can provide you with a geographical list of clubs to find ones in your area. Contact them at the above address.

Registry Organizations

Registry organizations register purebred dogs. The American Kennel Club is the oldest and largest in this country, and currently recognizes over 130 breeds. The United Kennel Club registers some breeds the AKC doesn't (including the American Pit Bull Terrier and the Miniature Fox Terrier) as well as many of the same breeds. The others included here are for your reference; the AKC can provide you with a list of foreign registries.

American Kennel Club
51 Madison Avenue
New York, NY 10010

United Kennel Club (UKC)
100 E. Kilgore Road
Kalamazoo, MI 49001-5598

American Dog Breeders Assn.
P.O. Box 1771
Salt Lake City, UT 84110
(Registers American Pit Bull Terriers)

Canadian Kennel Club
89 Skyway Avenue
Etobicoke, Ontario
Canada M9W 6R4

National Stock Dog Registry
P.O. Box 402
Butler, IN 46721
(Registers working stock dogs)

Orthopedic Foundation for Animals (OFA)
2300 E. Nifong Blvd.
Columbia, MO 65201-3856
(Hip registry)

Activity Clubs

Write to these organizations for information on the activities they sponsor.

American Kennel Club
51 Madison Avenue
New York, NY 10010
(Conformation Shows, Obedience Trials, Field
Trials and Hunting Tests, Agility, Canine Good

Citizen, Lure Coursing, Herding, Tracking,
Earthdog Tests, Coonhunting.)

United Kennel Club
100 E. Kilgore Road
Kalamazoo, MI 49001-5598
(Conformation Shows, Obedience Trials, Agility,
Hunting for Various Breeds, Terrier Trials and
more.)

North American Flyball Assn.
1342 Jeff St.
Ypsilanti, MI 48198

International Sled Dog Racing Assn.
P.O. Box 446
Norman, ID 83848-0446

North American Working Dog Assn., Inc.
Southeast Kreisgruppe
P.O. Box 833
Brunswick, GA 31521

Trainers

Association of Pet Dog Trainers
P.O. Box 3734
Salinas, CA 93912
(408) 663–9257

American Dog Trainers' Network
161 West 4th St.
New York, NY 10014
(212) 727–7257

**National Association of Dog Obedience
Instructors**
2286 East Steel Rd.
St. Johns, MI 48879

Beyond the
Basics

Associations

American Dog Owners Assn.
1654 Columbia Tpk.
Castleton, NY 12033
(Combats anti-dog legislation)

Delta Society
P.O. Box 1080
Renton, WA 98057-1080
(Promotes the human/animal bond through
pet-assisted therapy and other programs)

Dog Writers Assn. of America (DWAA)
Sally Cooper, Secy.
222 Woodchuck Ln.
Harwinton, CT 06791

National Assn. for Search and Rescue (NASAR)
P.O. Box 3709
Fairfax, VA 22038

Therapy Dogs International
6 Hilltop Road
Mendham, NJ 07945

All I Really
Need to Know
I Learned in
Sunday School

Cliff Schimmels

VICTOR BOOKS®

A DIVISION OF SCRIPTURE PRESS PUBLICATIONS INC.
USA CANADA ENGLAND

Library of Congress Cataloging-in-Publication Data

Schimmels, Cliff.
  All I really need to know I learned in Sunday School / Cliff
Schimmels.
        p.   cm.
      ISBN 0-89693-906-5
      1. Sunday schools. I. Title.
    BV1521.S35 1991
    268—dc20   91-15460
                                                       CIP

1 2 3 4 5 6 7 8 9 10 Printing/Year 95 94 93 92 91

CONTENTS

The little girl who sat on her grandma's lap brought laughter to her life.

"Grandma, in Sunday School I learned that Jesus lives in my heart." And then she showed her grandma where, with her little hand pressed firmly.

"That's good," the grandma said, "but how do you know that?"

The little girl pressed even more firmly and exclaimed, "I can feel Him jump!"

A child's understanding, a child's feelings, and a child's precious soul! That's the stuff of Sunday School.

We talk of institutions and programs, of curriculum and structure. We talk of class roles and growth trends, of evangelism and outreach. But we remember the people.

The names you remember are different than mine. The events and settings vary; yet, our memories are a

7

great deal alike because the people have so much in common . . . the teacher who stayed up late at night and made lessons from homemade materials; the kid sitting beside me who got his tongue twisted and brought new insight to a familiar passage; the leader who taught you to sing the song that leaps up still in your mind and mouth at the most unusual times — these are Sunday School.

And to those teachers and leaders and kids in my memories and yours, to the parents who dressed us and got us there and then quizzed us when we got home, to the little girl with Jesus jumping in her heart, and to the teacher who taught her almost that, I offer my thanks.

Cliff Schimmels
Wheaton, Illinois
1991

The Lesson of
THE UNBELIEVABLE

"WHAT DID YOU LEARN IN SUNDAY SCHOOL?" a father asked his son.

With a shrug of his shoulders and the tone of a child who has often been so questioned, the young boy said, "She told us about Moses crossing the Red Sea."

"Oh," the father inquired with eagerness, "what did she say?"

The boy paused only for a second and began the narrative. "Well, it seems like this fellow Israel had a whole bunch of children who were being held hostage by this guy Pharaoh. Well, old Moses got mad about that and went to this guy Pharaoh and gave this ultimatum. He warned him that if he didn't let those people go, he would be in big trouble. So Pharaoh said, 'Okay, you can leave.' Then Moses loaded all Israel's children in big buses and started off.

"Well, old Pharaoh thought about what he had done and changed his mind. He called out his army and tanks and half-tracks and big guns and began chasing old Moses.

11

"When Moses and all those children got to the Red Sea, they knew they were trapped and had to do something. So they decided to sandbag that old Sea. They sandbagged two sides all the way across. Then they got centrifugal pumps and pumped all the water out so that they could go through on the seabed.

"But they weren't finished. They put big explosives all through those sandbags, and when Pharaoh's army and machines started down through the Sea, the Children of Israel detonated those explosives with this remote device over on the other shore, blew up the sandbags, and destroyed Pharaoh's army."

"Wait a minute," the father protested with deep concern. "Is that the way she told the story?"

"Naw," said the boy with another shrug. "But if I told you the story the way she did, you'd never believe it."

And that's the first lesson of Sunday School. You have to learn to believe the unbelievable.

The curriculum is filled with such stories. The sea parted, the walls fell down, the clothes didn't wear out, the sun stood still, the lame man walked, the fishnets didn't break, and the virgin gave birth.

The whole church is filled with the stories of the unbelievable. Mrs. Metcalf had polio when she was a little girl. The doctors said she would never walk again, but now she doesn't even limp. Mr. Robinson was once a brawler and a drunk, but now he isn't.

Sunday School is about both kinds of stories because it's about the power of God at work in ordinary people.

For me, Sunday School is more than a refreshing experience. In the Sunday School stories, past and present, is the sap of my spiritual fervor.

In recent years, I have come to believe that the natural passages of life turn us all into auto-biographers. It is during these landmark or crises times that we remember our own histories—who we are and how we got to be this way.

Not long ago, I crossed a pleasant passage and gained a new name. I became someone's "Grandpa," and from this joy, I have found it de-lightfully necessary to make a mental list of all those times and people who have contributed to my being and becoming. I owe them all my gratitude. But in the midst of remembering moments complex and simple, of remembering lessons painful and pleasant, I have most frequently caught myself recalling Sun-day School. From earliest boyhood to last week, the memories flow and tumble, fleeting from year to year, and even decade to decade.

Some of those great lessons I caught at first im-pact, but others I didn't comprehend until that spe-cial moment years later when, during my quiet con-templation, God gave me insight and brought meaning to a memory.

It's through such moments that I have come to see special significance and truth in a popular title re-phrased to meet my personal pilgrimage. Everything I really need to know, I learned in Sunday School.

But the big lesson was that I learned to believe the unbelievable.

The Lesson of
THE BACK ROOM

THE OTHER DAY a woman called to invite me to come to her church to speak to the Little Children's Sunday School Class.

I accepted immediately. Speaking to the Little Children's Sunday School Class is top priority with me. I seize any opportunity that has possibility of "touching the future," as one teacher put it. Besides that, my mind works at the level of little children.

Because I had never been to her church before, the caller volunteered to meet me at the front door so that she could help me find the classroom.

"I don't think that will be necessary," I answered as politely as I could, but with a ring of confidence that surprised even me. "I'm sure I can find it on my own. I'll just go to the very back room."

There was silence on her end for a moment; then she chuckled. "You're right, but how did you know?" she asked, in the kind of tone that assured me that she really didn't expect an answer.

She was fortunate to communicate that tone. I do

14

have an answer to her question, but it would take me
at least an hour to deliver it. After all, it took me a
lifetime to gather it, and I still get a bit emotional
with any provocation to recount why I know where
the Little Children's Sunday School Class is.

Any time we ponder such matters as this and think
of how we know what we know, and how we got to
be who we are, the word *first* becomes one of the
major terms of our vocabulary. It keeps popping up
everywhere.

One of the common activities of personality as-
sessment is to recall our very first memory. We hold
special our first bout with romance. God sent word
to the church at Ephesus that He was upset with
them because they had forsaken their first love.

In matters spiritual and religious, our very first
experiences are not only the openings into the new
and abundant life, but they also become doormen
supervising and directing the entrance of all subsequent experiences. The special places with their own
special sights and sounds and odors live active lives
in our storehouse of memories long after other memories have faded into oblivion.

With those first impressions right at the threshold
of our consciousness, we remember how Sunday
School should look, and we remember how Sunday
School should smell. And now years and decades
and scores later, our senses will catch a faint whiff of
the stuff of first experiences, and all the memories
will come tumbling back as fresh as on the day of
origin. We catch a quick glance or smell, and we say,

"Now that's Sunday School."

In the same way, the special people with their quirks and habits and talents and smiles and tears become the people appropriate to Sunday School experiences at all times and places, and we find ourselves hoping that our children and grandchildren can have a teacher just like our very first and can know classmates like those in our first class.

Those first places and people become prototypes. Years later, we may become bold enough to experiment with alternate structures and places, but we experiment with the security of the memory of the first.

I first found the happiness of learning about the Lord in a small country church which sat serenely in the middle of a fertile valley. The hills which served as sentries both on the east and west were aesthetically decorated with red dirt, green grass, and frequent outcroppings of white gypsum. The valley, long and slender, was like a beehive of plant life buzzing with cotton, corn, wheat, and alfalfa.

The church building itself was unmistakably *the* church building of the community. It was stately and tall, painted white and well-kept. Built on the only little rise in the valley, it could be seen from almost every farm home, as if it were a standing symbol of centrality. Even strangers driving through the community could glance in that direction and know immediately that this was the church.

As I remember it through boy eyes, it was a gigantic building, with rooms spacious and plentiful; in truth, it was one big room with a network of curtains which could be pulled in a variety of ways to create separate spaces which could be imagined into rooms with the individual traits and flaws which make rooms significant in our memories.

For learning, our Sunday School was divided into two general sections — adults and children. At the very beginning of each Sunday morning, the curtains were pulled to divide the church into two rooms where each group had a general opening exercise where we sang together, had a short introduction to the lesson, took up the offering, each put money in the birthday bank one Sunday a year, and prayed.

Then the back part where the children met was further divided into three more classrooms as sturdy as curtains and imaginations could make them, one for the school-age boys, one for school-age girls, and one for the little children — those who had not yet learned to read. Of course, the little children went into the very back room. I'm sure there was a reason for that in the beginning; but even after the original reason had been lost somewhere in the passing of the years, and the new reason had become "just because," the little children still met in the back room.

The people of our church and of my first experiences came from all over the valley, and they came in great hordes. Not long ago I saw the actual statistics and realized that the record attendance for that great horde was sixty-seven on a Sunday when we had a special preacher coming. But sixty-seven is a relative number, and to a boy in the midst of his first experience, that was a great horde.

Most of those people had been born in the valley and had lived there all their lives, and they brought to our church the riches of diversity. There are those who would tell us that there can't possibly be any diversity in a crowd of people who live in the same spot and do the same things for a living and have similar last names.

But I learned early that diversity is the product of perspective and not circumstance. Each person there had a unique relationship with God and a unique relationship with the world, and that uniqueness provided enough diversity to hold me in a state of awe as I sat in classes or listened to the conversations, or discovered the majesty and reality of God during the open testimony times. Regardless of what experiences and teachers I might know in the years to follow, I shall never forget some of those early lessons that those people taught me from their diversity.

Mrs. Smith was in charge of the children's section, conducted the opening exercise, and taught the school-age girls. She was a pleasant woman who could be firm. Perhaps that is why she was so good at what she did. She had a look that could control us and a heart big enough to hold us.

Mrs. Smith was an expert in the Epistles. Regardless of the nature of the lesson for the day, she could find something from one of Paul's letters that would not only relate but contribute to our understanding. From her I learned to love his letters.

Mrs. Murphy, who taught the school-age boys, was an expert in the Old Testament, particularly the history part. She not only knew the names of all the kings, but she even knew in what order they came and whether they were good or bad.

From her as much as from any teacher I have ever had anywhere or anytime, I learned the lesson of the reality of the past. Each Sunday I came to realize that the people of the Bible were more than fictional characters in fairy tales. They were real. They ate and had children and had disputes with their children, and they cried and died.

After all these years, I will sometimes flip through those pages of my Bible which are still a bit slick with newness in far-off spots such as 1 Chronicles, and I will remember Mrs. Murphy, and I will resent my schedule which will not permit me the hours needed to relive and learn.

Mrs. Henderson, the other person in our children's section, owned the back corner. She taught the little children and was synonymous with that back corner. Since she had walls plus a curtain, she decorated with permanent posters and charts, and had class longer than anybody else.

Mrs. Henderson was the church grandmother. Some of the children were actually her very own grandchildren, but the rest of us didn't know which ones they were. She was everyone's grandmother who brought cookies and spiritual concern.

Mrs. Henderson loved the prophecy part of the Bible, and was a scholar in that area. Even during the war years when some items of luxury were scarce, Mrs. Henderson had a battery and her radio worked. So she listened and brought the rest of us reports, not only of the news of the world, but of the wisdom of the radio preachers who in those days were quite concerned about biblical prophecy.

Sometimes as we get older, it's hard to discern what impact some event or some person years before has had. To this day, I am not sure I know the significance of why I remember Mrs. Smith's purple dress, or Mrs. Murphy's sense of humor, or the mole on Mrs. Henderson's chin. Recollections of other people that have come between then and now have faded into faintness. Maybe I remember because they were the first, and they remind me of something bigger and more precious.

My prayer is that Jesus won't ever find a need to send to me the reprimand that he had to deliver to those people at Ephesus. To make sure that I don't lose the memory of the joy of the energy of that first love, I will give it the structure of the lessons of people and places who filled that time for me. And that's how I know where the little children meet.

The Lesson of
SINGING BEFORE STUDYING

SUNDAY SCHOOL CEREMONIES come in two types. There are those which are temporary. They come and go, drifting in from season to season or year to year or director to director.

But there are those ceremonies which are permanent. They span seasons and years and generations and endure attacks and diseases and pressures.

These permanent ceremonies come in two types. There are those which are authenticated and documented by Scripture, doctrinal position, or even history. There are others, however, which are permanent on the very convincing logic that this is the way it is supposed to be.

The order of service falls into that last category. Well, perhaps there is some flexibility in places in the agenda, but there is one permanent principle which has survived all generations and all tests and all trends: You must sing before you study.

There may actually be some biblical support for this. The people in Old Testament days sang at some unusual times. Moses and his people sang out of happiness after they had safely escaped across the Red Sea. David responded to almost all of the human conditions by breaking out into song. He sang when he lost; he sang when he won; he sang when God was happy with him and when He wasn't.

In Sunday School, we sang the first thing. Whether there is significant biblical support for this or not, it served a very real purpose. It woke us up.

Of all the words which we could use to describe that opening song service, the most accurate one would be *hearty.* We sang as if maybe we thought God Himself was a little sleepy on Sunday morning and needed a jolt of shrill sounds.

In Sunday School singing, the whole body must participate. Some of the songs had hand gestures that were as much a part of the song as the words and the tune. No adult who grew up in Sunday School can sing "Deep and Wide" with his hands in his pockets. Another song with hearty hand gestures was, "I'm In Right, Out Right, Up Right, Down Right, Happy All the Time." That one was not only loud and vigorous, but it also required a good deal of room.

Perhaps that's why we Americans seem to need so much personal body space. We grew up singing action songs in Sunday School. When the songs didn't have gestures, we would often invent them, just to show that we were participating.

For the opening ceremonies at our Sunday School, we had piano accompaniment with our singing, but on a limited basis. The only person who could play was Mary Wade, and she could play only in one flat. So Mrs. Smith had to stay up late every Saturday night to make the right selections, and we never got any free sing time.

In those days, when the overhead projector was just so much science fiction, teaching the words of a new song was something of a trial of special gifts. But since Mrs. Smith was both clever and determined, she would write the words with crayons on backs of the rolls of wallpaper that she had left over from decorating. That way, we didn't get the words on some flat surface, but they sort of unrolled in front of us as if we were player pianos responding to cardboard programs.

For me, the song service period was a time for sore ribs. That was not because I sang heartily but because I sang off-key and someone was always poking me. My ability to sing off-key earned me quite a reputation. The kid beside me would stop occasionally and blurt out, "Clifford's singing off-key," and everybody would stare and giggle and still keep going, "I'm in right, out right, up right, down right, happy all the time." But this didn't bother Mrs. Smith. She would nod at me as if it were all right for me to sing off-key as long as I was hearty about it. Of course, at Christmas programs and Rally Days she did ask me just to move my mouth and not let any sound come out. My singing earned me my boyhood nickname, Off-Key Cliff, and I still wear it as a badge of honor.

In spite of my personal successes in the song service, I heartily endorse the principle. Singing before studying is not only a logical order, but it seems to be a natural one as well. Singing stimulates the body, mind, and soul, both for the participant and for the listener. Music, even music that is more hearty than aesthetic, soothes, calms, awakens and refreshes. After having sung together, we could join in and study with a greater sense of genuineness and with the feeling that we were a part of the community; we were not quite as isolated as we had been just a few minutes earlier.

Through my personal research of having thought about this little principle for almost fifty years, I have concluded that singing before studying is still one of the best things we do in Sunday School. I am, in fact, such a strong supporter that I am trying to discover ways to launch this order into other areas of human assembly.

Just for starters, let's think about a court of law. Everybody stands when the judge enters the room and goes to his elevated postion. How would it be if just before he sat down, he would lift his arms in those flowing sleeves and lead everybody in a rousing chorus. I think I would recommend that they all sing,

> "My hope is built on nothing less
> than Jesus' love and righteousness. . . .
> On Christ, the solid rock I stand,
> all other ground is sinking sand."

Such a reminder would assure everybody of what justice is. Just maybe after the people had all sung together, they wouldn't get so angry with each other during the court proceedings.

Another place where this principle might have merit would be a space launch. Those are tense times anyway, and a little pre-blast-off singing might do a lot to release anxiety and bring unity. In that case, two songs would seem appropriate, "How Great Thou Art," and "Amazing Grace."

As a person educated in Sunday School ceremonies, I would like to see more singing at summit conferences. Have you ever noticed how weary the participants look, as if they would really rather be back in their rooms taking a nap? If they could just pause in the middle of all their serious deliberations to jump into a chorus or two of "Do Lord" and finish it off with a vigorous rendition of "Deep and Wide," they would feel so refreshed.

I know that I still do at Sunday School, sore ribs and all.

The Lesson of
THE VACANT
FRONT ROW

IN THE THEATER, Front Row Center is the best seat in the house. In the classroom, the eager scholars, the overachievers and those who think their cuteness will appeal to the teacher fight for the front row. At the major leaguer's autograph party, people scramble and trample to get to the front.

In church the front row is unoccupied. I always wondered why that is. At first, I thought that there were doctrinal reasons, but when I got old enough to visit other churches, I learned that this was not just a fact of our local congregation or denomination but was far more global.

Although we didn't know its source or origin, the students in our Sunday School class knew fully the Law of the Vacant Front Row, and we attempted to abide by it in both letter and spirit. But that presented a problem. Ours was a poor church, and we didn't have all that many chairs. Sometimes when we had preaching all day and then dinner on the grounds with large crowds, people would even bring chairs from home just to have a place to sit.

In our class, that shortage was acute. There were just enough chairs for each of us to have one, so during the final prayer of opening exercise, the aggressive would begin to lean and shuffle toward the curtain which designated our Sunday School room, so that on the Amen they could make a break for the second and third rows. The rest of us would straggle in, fight those already there, lose, and wind up sitting on the floor during class. But the front row was still silently and reverently vacant.

Mrs. Murphy wasn't pleased with that arrangement. I think she must have found that teaching boys the purpose of memorizing the books of the Bible in order, while they were wrestling on the floor, was in itself a study in incongruity.

But Mrs. Murphy had a natural teaching gift. This means that she was smarter than boys, even at their own game. She devised a solution. Mrs. Murphy rearranged the room. She placed one lone chair up front right in the middle. Behind it she placed a full row of seats; then she told us that the one lone chair was the front row and the full row was technically the second row. That made sense to us, so we filled all the seats except the one that constituted the front row. After that we all had a seat, except for the Henderson boy who was always late anyway.

Although we accepted her new style of interior decorating, being typical boys we were a bit uncomfortable with the appearance of the strangeness, so we responded with typical boy rebellion. We asked

27

questions—tons and tons of questions. Well, actually we didn't ask a wide variety of questions, but we asked the same question over and over again, and each time we asked it, we had the tone in our voices as if we were the first persons ever to think it, much less to ask.

"Why is the room this way?" "Whose chair is that?" "Who's supposed to sit up there?" "Why is that one seat in the front?"

After Mrs. Murphy had either waited until the level of learning anxiety was appropriate, or had gone totally beserk with all the questions—I couldn't tell which, she decided to turn that one lone chair into a lesson—a powerful and memorable lesson which surely not a single one of us ever forgot.

One morning at about the hundredth repetition of the same question or a reasonable paraphrase, Mrs. Murphy paused, put down her lesson leaflet, and opened her Bible. "Listen carefully," she told us, "and I will explain once and only once about this empty chair." With that announcement, she drew immediate attention, not silent attention, but attention amidst the rustle, because we were excited to get to know this.

Then she began to read to us. From the book of 2 Kings, one of her favorite books, she read this neat story about a great guy. It concluded, "As they were walking along and talking together, suddenly a chariot of fire and horses of fire appeared and separated the two of them and Elijah went up to heaven in a whirlwind."

That one simple reading provoked a barrage of questions which she answered with an eagerness that showed us that she really enjoyed telling this story to a group of boys who would appreciate it. But as the questions quieted down and as we sat imagining this great scene in our minds, she explained that to this day, Jewish people still expect Elijah to return. Sometimes when they have special feasts and special programs, they reserve a chair at the table to show that they are expecting him to return.

"This chair up here," Mrs. Murphy explained to us, once and for always, "is reserved for Elijah." And she picked up her lesson leaflet and started the class again.

I appreciated the explanation because it clarifies one of the great mysteries in life and worship. That's why churches keep the front row vacant. They want Elijah to have his choice, and from the best seats in the house too.

The Lesson of "YES, MA'AM"

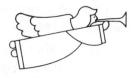

AT OUR HOUSE, we always got our Sunday papers on Saturday night. Out where we lived there was no delivery, so we picked up the paper when we were in town.

There was one advantage to that—we had read the comics by the time we got to Sunday School the next morning. That little opportunity provided one of the highlights of the week. With utter delight, I could sit around and tell the rest of the kids what they could expect. I took special joy in telling the story right up to the punch line and then quitting just in time to make everyone beg for the finish.

In those days one of the our favorite topics in the comics was science fiction, and frequently, the Sunday morning conversation got around to such wild futuristic speculations as wrist radios and remote control devices. Of course, these were only things of the imagination, too far from reality to be taken with any seriousness, but it was still fun to chat about and to speculate on what life would be like in that way-off future time called the twenty-first century.

One day, right in the middle of our dreaming, Leroy Brady, who buttoned the top button of his sport shirt and did arithmetic problems in his head, startled us all. "I plan to live in the twenty-first century," he boldly proclaimed, and the rest of us hissed and booed.

"Figure it out for yourself," he urged us. So we got the stub pencils they brought to our classroom after they were whittled too short to be used behind the pews anymore, and we figured it out in the margins of the weekly lesson leaflets.

That's when we discovered that most of us would be sixty-three years old when this world entered the twenty-first century. At that time, sixty-three seemed old, but we knew some people who had reached that advanced stage in life, and we decided it really wasn't beyond expectation.

The next problem in our conversation was how we might achieve longevity and actually live to see the future for ourselves. And that's when Mrs. Murphy came to teach. Mrs. Murphy was a good teacher. She studied her lesson well. But she was also a good teacher because she studied the boys well. This day, she sensed something deep was in the air, and she wisely chose to take care of that before she proceeded with the map of Paul's Second Missionary Journey.

"So you want to live to be old?" she asked us, and winced just a bit when we mentioned sixty-three. "Well, let me tell you the way to live a long time."

And we gathered around close as if we didn't want this secret information to slip out to extraterrestrial spies who might be lurking. Besides, Mrs. Murphy was about sixty-three herself. Maybe she really did have a secret. With ears open and eyes bulging like so many bullfrogs, we waited for the formula.

Sensing the seriousness of moment, she bent over and whispered, but loud enough for us all to hear, "Say 'Yes, Ma'am.' " And we waited in the quiet for the rest of it, but there wasn't anymore. She stood up straight, grinned at us and started speaking normally again.

Were we disappointed! We were primed for a secret right out of the science fiction of the comics, and she gave us this. We expressed our disappointment. Loudly and with enthusiasm that grows exponentially in gatherings of boys, we told her of our disappointment.

She laid her finger to her lips to gain silence and asked, "What do you say when your mother tells you to go outside and gather the eggs?"

"Yes, Mother, we will," we all answered in unison with a molasses response, because we knew that this was the kind of answer they expect you to give in Sunday School.

But Mrs. Murphy didn't buy it. "No, what do you really say?" And she left us alone with our own thoughts as we remembered outbursts of disrespect and even rudeness. Then she added, "You really need to learn to say, 'Yes, Ma'am,' and maybe you'll see the twenty-first century."

She opened her Bible and read to an attentive class of young boys, "Honor your father and your mother, so that you may live long in the land the Lord your God is giving you." Then she added her own comment. "It starts with learning to say a simple 'Yes, Ma'am.' "

Through the years, I have bought the best tapes, read the best books, attended the best seminars and sat under the best teachers in an attempt to learn how to live in a way that would please God. But Mrs. Murphy's prescription still makes about as much sense as anything I have heard since then. "It starts with learning to say a simple " 'Yes, Ma'am.' "

The Lesson of
THE SHOES

WHILE WE WERE GROWING UP, we always had two pairs of shoes. They were named Everyday Shoes and Sunday School Shoes.

We wore Everyday Shoes everyday, and they always took a licking. In those shoes, we kicked clods, climbed trees, chased cows, and did the chores.

We also wore Everyday Shoes to school, so they became a representation of the kind of day we were having. Scuff marks on the right toe reminded us of the joy of getting to the bus stop a few minutes early and having time to engage in a round or two of Kick the Can with brothers or sisters.

Scuff marks on the left toe announced progress in skill development because we could use both feet to kick the can.

Those were the messages we received from our eyes. Our nose had another story to tell. On some mornings, chores did not go perfectly. On most mornings, chores did not go perfectly. Of all the things pigs are, cooperative is not on the list, and so feeding the pigs was always an adventure frequently documented in after-the-event odors.

But nervous cows could be the most troublesome. They would kick and stomp and swish, and half the milk would wind up on Everyday Shoes instead of in the pail.

In the brisk chill of early morning, that wasn't much of a catastrophe; but about ten o'clock while we were sitting close to a warm radiator trying to learn mental discipline by mastering the sequential steps of long division, that milk stain had a way of awakening the nose and stimulating memories of all mishaps already met that day.

Sunday was different. As usual, we would begin our day with our old friends, Everyday Shoes, but somewhere in the course of the morning would come that poignant moment when it was time to put on Sunday School Shoes.

That moment was like having a miniature Christmas each week. What anticipation! What excitement—to be able to slip our feet into elegance.

But Mother never trusted anticipation alone. That moment was always set in motion by parental reminder which all too often took on the needless tone of reprimand.

"Change your shoes," she would say, in a mood much like that in Indianapolis when the man says, "Start your engines." But before we could race into action, she would offer further explanation. "You don't want to wear those old filthy Everyday Shoes to Sunday School. Jesus is watching."

That's how the transformation occurred every Sunday. Putting on those shoes had special significance. They not only changed our appearance, but they changed our character. They brought an odd combination of reverence and joy to our lives.

The demands of temptation were still there — the need to giggle when somebody burped during prayer, the need to push when the line to the crayon box got out of control, the need to daydream when the lesson was too long.

But dealing with all that temptation was a bit easier while wearing special shoes that reminded us, "Jesus is watching." Being good brought a special pleasure.

However, the day inevitably came when those two pairs of shoes produced confusion and anxiety. Right in the middle of doing something really important such as kicking a clod or chasing a cow, the sole would break lose on one of the Everyday Shoes and would flap about like the tongue of a collie drinking from the creek. We would then surgically remove the offending part and stuff cardboard inside until we could get to town and buy new shoes.

We never bought new Everyday Shoes. The new shoes were named Sunday School Shoes, and what used to be Sunday School Shoes were reassigned and rechristened Everyday Shoes.

That's when the theological confusion began. Wearing those shoes had always brought a sense of reverence to our existence. We knew that Jesus was watching. Mother told us that. And we could curb most of our normal impulses for the duration. But now what did we do?

For three days after that transition, we walked around in our Puritan faces and modified behavior, living constantly under the ever watchful eye of Jesus.

Now that middle age and middle class have invaded my life, I have three pairs of shoes and I haven't designated any one as Sunday School Shoes. But I have learned to live with the dilemma.

Mother's reminder was accurate; it just needed extending. Jesus is watching while we are wearing Sunday School Shoes. But He also is watching when we are wearing Everyday Shoes, or even going barefoot, for that matter.

Jesus told us this Himself when He said, "And surely I am with you always, to the very end of the age."

That isn't a threat. It's a promise.

The Lesson of
THE OLD MARE

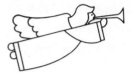

ONE OF THE MOST IMPORTANT LESSONS I ever learned in Sunday School, and one that I find myself using frequently, was a lesson my father taught me — and he wasn't even there.

One day I rode The Old Mare to Sunday School. No, the capital letters are not mistakes. That was the horse's name. At our house, we didn't stay awake late at night trying to name our animals. We had a dog named Dawg. We had a cow named The Heifer. When that animal got to be twenty-one years old and one of the oldest cows in captivity, we still called her The Heifer.

As I said, I rode The Old Mare to Sunday School. In those days, riding a horse to Sunday School was the equivalent of taking the limo today. We lived three miles away, and on most Sundays we had to walk. On some Sundays, we rode The Old Mare, but I had to ride with my older brother and sister, and that was more like going on the bus. It was faster than walking, but not much. And it was terribly crowded. I had to hang on tight just to keep from getting killed.

On this day, I rode The Old Mare by myself. We always had a rule at our house that when we rode a horse and tied her up for some time, we took the bridle off. Some folks' horses could drink through the bits, but our horses never could master that little art. We took the bridle off so The Old Mare could keep her tummy full of water, drinking from the tub out by the tree where we all tied our horses during Sunday School and church.

On the day of the big lesson, I dawdled some on my way. Actually, I stopped to chase a coyote, and when I finally got to Sunday School, I could tell that I was almost late. One of the Henderson kids was already scampering across the lawn, so I knew I was in trouble. I didn't want to be late to class. I didn't want to be embarrassed, walking in behind a Henderson, and also I was worried that God would mind. That's when I made a big mistake. I didn't bother to take the bridle off. I just rushed into Sunday School and started singing and praying and studying as if I were holy.

But I couldn't get my mind off The Old Mare, standing out under that tree in the warm April wind without any means of getting at the water. And the thought pestered me all through Sunday School, all through the song service, all through the preacher's message which was particularly long this day and seemed even longer with me trying to concentrate while thinking about that horse. And if that wasn't bad enough, we had Communion that day.

We never had Communion except on the Thursday night before Easter, but that Sunday we had Communion. I wasn't really attentive because I was thinking about poor Old Mare. I tried to get my mind off her by remembering Bible verses, but the only thing I could think of was verses which pertained to this. Wrestling with my guilt, I might have paraphrased a bit as I recalled such past lessons as, "When the ox is in the ditch, common sense is more important than laws." Or, "Do unto your horse as you would have your horse do unto you."

And I thought of the day I would stand before Jesus and He would say, "I was thirsty and you didn't even take the bridle off."

Frightened and guilt-ridden, as soon as I heard "Amen," I leaped out of my seat and ran out to that tree prepared to take the bridle off and, like Zaccheus, make restitution for my past sins. But, alas, the other horses had already drunk all the water in the tub, and I had to ride The Old Mare all the way home in the heat and wind.

When I got home, I rode her right straight to the tank; I pulled the bridle off, and she started to drink. And she drank and drank and drank. She drank with such force that her sides would heave, and she'd snort water out her nose. Then she would pause, lift her head up, and stare at me with those sad eyes of hers and drink some more.

My father came out of the house, walked out to where we were, stood and watched and didn't say a word. I bowed my head and waited for the on-slaught, the almost welcome reprimand that I was going to get for my sins. But he didn't say a word. He just watched. When The Old Mare had finally managed to restore her system, we started to the barn, and my father came along side of me. "Did you learn anything in Sunday School today?" he asked in a tone made threatening by its calmness.

"Yes, Sir," I said with my head down so I couldn't look at him. And that was the last time he ever mentioned it.

A few years ago, God called me to deliver the Sunday sermon at a nearby church. About eight o'clock on Saturday night, I sat down with my commentaries and seven translations of the Scripture to put the finishing touches on what had the potential of being an oratorical and theological masterpiece.

Just then the phone rang. Our friends' son was ill at youth camp about three hours away, and they were very worried. Realizing that they were too up-set to go alone, my wife and I loaded them into our car and drove the three hours up, spent two hours nursing him, and drove the three hours home.

We got home just in time for me to shower, change my shirt, and go off to church to deliver the great "Unfinished Sermon."

I probably should put a fitting ending on this by telling you that the sermon went off beautifully, but that's not true. It lacked depth and coherence and illustration and energy. And the congregation knew it.

At the end, I stood at the door and shook hands with gracious people who awkwardly fished for something nice to say about the homiletic flop. But while I stood there, I remembered that day years ago when I didn't take the bridle off. I remembered the lesson I had learned, and I realized why I had made my decision the night before.

They also serve God who water horses and take distraught parents on an overnight trip.

The Lesson of
THE RIGHT ORDER

GENESIS, EXODUS, Leviticus, Numbers, Deuteronomy . . . Mrs. Murphy made us learn the books of the Bible in order. I guess we should have seen it coming. In those days, that assignment was as much a part of Sunday School as singing before you study. Every student in every class in every church in the world, I suppose, learned to say the books of the Bible in order. But like so many things in life, even though it was inevitable, it was still unexpected.

I think she planned it that way. She wanted us to spend our energy learning the books in order, instead of dreading to have to learn them in order. One day she came to class and said simply, "In two weeks, you will have to recite the books of the Bible in order."

Her announcement came so quickly and easily that we sat stunned. We didn't even have time to bombard her with the customary questions such as, "How are we going to be tested? Do you take off for pronunciation? How many chances do we get?"

In the midst of the surprise and confusion which stifled our creativity, we came up with only one of the usually required questions, "Why are we doing this?" She grinned and said, "It'll be good for you. It'll make your brains grow."

When I got home that noon, my father, fulfilling one of the first requirements of fatherhood, asked, "What did you learn in Sunday School today?"

I answered, "We have to learn the books of the Bible in order." Now that I have become a father, I realize how that answer doesn't quite fit the question which was asked. I'm sure my father was hoping for a discourse on some significant Bible event or character, complete with a description and critical commentary. Now that I'm a Sunday School teacher, I'm sure that she taught us that too. But that isn't what we learned. We learned the assignment, so my answer was actually the correct one.

"Well, good," my father said. "That'll make your brain grow," and he went back to reading the paper.

The next day in school, we held the Sunday School debriefing the very first thing, and because this was a time when I was in my "front row" period, I was the first one questioned. Mrs. Foster looked straight at me and asked, "What did you learn in Sunday School yesterday?"

And I said, "We have to learn the books of the Bible in order."

And Mrs. Foster said, "Well, good. That'll make your brain grow," and with that she went on to the kid behind me.

With no apparent sympathy in sight, I decided that I had no choice but to get on with the task. After all, how tough could this be? There were only sixty-six names to learn, that much I knew, and it seemed that if every adult in the world had learned the books of the Bible in order, surely I could.

But I found this learning activity to be one of the most difficult assignments I have ever had. It put me into sections of the Bible where I felt like Balboa exploring territory where no human being had ever been before. Perhaps it was the big words and the unusual ways I had to twist my tongue to try to copy what my ear heard when my big brother said them for me. Perhaps it was just the nature of the order itself, but I found the task extremely difficult.

Some books were easier than others. The first five came quickly, but the section with Micah, Nahum, Habakkuk, and Zephaniah required complete concentration, hours and hours of repetition, and the frustration of trial and error. It wasn't just these obscure spots that caused trouble. I had a time with Ephesians, Colossians, Philippians, and Galatians too. I also got fooled in those places where I thought it would be easy. I liked those spots where there is a First and a Second, and breezed through those feeling almost as if I were cheating or least getting a bonus point. But then I ran into the First, Second, and Third, and had to work at remembering which was which.

When the day of oral exams came, I was prepared but not confident. Since the testing was to be in public and we had the luxury of learning from everyone who had gone before, I prayed that God would allow me not to be first. He heard and answered. We drew numbers out of the box, and I was fourth. That was the right number. I would have the value of listening to those earlier ones and still be far enough up into the list that I wouldn't be worn out when it came my time.

As the three students in front of me recited, I listened, but only with one ear because I was still cramming. When it came my turn, I made it all the way up to the trouble spot of those last books of the Old Testament, and with concentration and by reading Mrs. Murphy's facial response, I made it all the way through without a single mistake. I was so pleased with myself. In fact, I was proud. I started into the New Testament and said, "Matthew, Luke, John," and those who had already finished and were listening more than the others caught my mistake and laughed. I was embarrassed and flustered. Mrs. Murphy only smiled and said, "That's all right. Go on." But that was the problem. I couldn't go on. When they laughed, I lost my rhythm and couldn't remember where I was at all. Again, she saw my plight and said, "That's all right. Just start over again."

So I did. "Genesis, Exodus, Leviticus, Numbers . . ."

It's funny how little things become your reputation. You could live your whole life being brilliant and diligent and talented, and one slip of the tongue

becomes your legacy. One moment of misunder-
standing and people will remember you forever. I
thought that was a minor thing at the time, but it
hasn't turned out that way. That's part of the lore of
the valley now. People tell their grandchildren about
me, or at least about the day I had to start over
again. At reunions, this is the remembered topic.
And I thought I was doing what she had asked.

Despite that, I still believe in the assignment. If I
could make a prescription for all fourth graders in
this nation, I would have them learn the books of the
Bible in order. I do think the reason is greater than
pure spite. . . . "If I had to, so should they."

I have found that mastery to be one of the most
profitable pieces of mental machinery I possess. I am
fairly good in Sword Drill games, and I can find the
text when the preacher announces it. But it's deeper
than that. Knowing the books in order is an entryway
into the Scriptures themselves. We could be good
Bible scholars without knowing the right order, but
just having this knowledge is a reminder that we
should know and that we *can* know.

The other day, I read the local newspaper with an
intensity somewhere between casual and slightly interested, and I counted twenty-seven references to
the Bible. I found myself feeling sorry for people
who don't know the books of the Bible in order or
who don't have some other tool for studying the
greatest Book of all. They obviously would have
missed those allusions, references, and analogies,
and their reading of the newspaper would have been

less than what it might have been.

It occurred to me that day that we actually cheat our children when we don't require them to learn the books of the Bible in order. Besides that, it would make their brains grow.

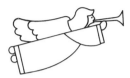

The Lesson of
THE BROKEN
CRAYONS

COLORING was not my favorite thing to do. It didn't even make the top ten. On a list of irregular duties and responsibilities, coloring was down around getting knots out of shoelaces when I was in a hurry to go swimming and pulling cockleburs out of cows' tails.

Just the thought of coloring in Sunday School was enough to haunt me awake at least twice every Saturday night with a jolt loud enough to wake up my brother and any other assorted animal life that happened to be sleeping in or around our bed.

The reason for my fear was justified — the result of a blending the natural and the theological.

In His infinite wisdom, God saw fit to make me an upside-down left-hander. Actually, I'm not so sure whether it was God's design or my childish invention born out of necessity to write with some hand. Since I didn't know the difference between left and right, the pencil just sort of wound up in my left hand, and I turned my hand upside down for better control.

That's how it happened. To some it might seem so very natural, but I still feel that it was providential, and all those people who have laughed at my penmanship through the years will someday answer for their sins.

My coloring was not only awkward but messy. And Sunday School coloring was the worst. Every Sunday morning there would come that dramatic moment in the lesson when Mrs. Murphy—or sometimes Mrs. Smith—would roll her eyes around the room, grin rather falsely, and exclaim, "Have you ever wondered what those people in your lesson today must have looked like?"

In later years as I have acquired a taste for big words, I have learned that educators call this moment and its subsequent activity "visualization." The teachers themselves call it "time off."

The reaction was always the same. All the other children would wiggle with glee, and I would sit in utter dread as the teacher distributed sheets of paper with faint outlines of the heroes of the day.

Then, amidst the wiggle, she would give the magic signal, "You may go get crayons now." And the herd would rush full speed ahead to the cigar boxes in which a giant assortment of crayons, present, past, and a long time ago were stored. Have you ever wondered what would have happened in those days to Sunday School, and elementary education in general if there had been no cigar boxes?

Of course, the aggressive ones would get to the boxes first and rummage with the intent of a shopper at a clearance sale until they found not only the choicest colors but also the longest and newest.

By the time the timid and the coloring haters got a turn to look, there remained only the stubby and broken bits of what used to be. Those broken pieces of color stuffed into my already awkward left hand squelched any Rembrandt fantasies I might have had.

Monochromatic assignments were at least manageable. Things like elephants and sheep and camels and Mt. Sinai allowed me to blob and smear without paying too much heed to that one artistic paradigm above all paradigms, "Stay within the lines."

But multicolored assignments with small spaces brought definition to the label "Fine Arts" and terror to my soul.

One day near Christmas, Mrs. Murphy told us about the wise men who came to visit the Baby Jesus. They were kings, actually, dressed in the richest and brightest colors of the day, and we should color them so.

Now, I ask you, have you ever tried to paint royalty with only an ancient piece of purple crayon?

I managed enough hand control to make the king's cloak purple, but I also managed to make his face purple too. When Mrs. Murphy and the aggressive coloring lovers all laughed and mocked, "Why is his face purple?" I explained that this wise man was happy. After all, he was the one who had brought the myrth.

Coloring poorly does have one serendipitous advantage. It causes one to develop a quick wit.

But this all changed when Edith came to our Sunday School. I never really knew where she came from. She just showed up one day, and about a year later, she disappeared.

Edith was not one of the aggressive ones. In fact, she was so unassuming that we would not even have known her name except that she had to wear a New Person name tag three weeks in a row.

On her first Sunday, when Mrs. Smith asked, "Is there anyone here for the first time?" Walter, who helped Mrs. Smith run things and always got the biggest crayon, pointed to Edith and shouted out loud, "I don't know that girl over there. I've never seen her before." So Edith got to wear the New Person name tag.

The second week she was there, we went through the very same ritual, but on the third Sunday after cheeky Walter said his piece, Mrs. Smith suddenly remembered that she had written the name "Edith" before, and after that, Edith didn't have to wear a New Person name tag.

When it came time to color, Edith didn't rush with the herd to the storage cabinet. She was so shy she was even behind me. Without a hint of frustration, she reached into the box and took one of the leftover bits. But what happened in the next few minutes revolutionized Sunday School art and the world in general. What Edith did was not only a thing of beauty but it has become a joy forever for all upside-down left-handers everywhere, and in so doing it has authenticated messages on Grecian urns.

With only a nub of a crayon in her hand, Edith proceeded to tear its paper away. She then placed the side of the crayon on the Walls of Jericho and began to move the flat edge around the design.

The result was breathtakingly beautiful. By pressing more firmly on the outside, she created a shading effect; and with the continuous motion, she eliminated the telltale blotches of children's art. And all the while, she stayed within the lines.

Besides that, she was the first one finished. When Mrs. Smith held up Edith's work for all to see and admire, the room was filled with another color, the green of aggressive kids shown up at their own game.

And the world laughed joyously.

After that, even the aggressive kids picked the broken crayons, but they could never reach Edith's level because she was the master.

Through the years, this lesson of Edith and the broken crayon has been good for me. Although I don't always achieve the full power of the insight, the image is still with me, still haunting me with memories of delight and the joy of flexibility.

How often life deals us a broken crayon!

The dentist says, "I'm sorry. This is not your normal, run-of-the-mill cavity. This one requires ROOT CANAL."

You're in a hurry to a very important meeting with a very important person when you spot that cheery sign, "Road Construction Ahead."

The salesman says, "If you can't afford this one, I

have another model almost as nice."

The boss asks, "Could you have it by Monday?"

That teenager who is your very own flesh and blood, your posterity and hope, has a total vocabulary of three phrases, "Everybody else will be there," "That's not fair," and "You don't trust me."

At such moments I remember the Sunday School lesson from the day when Edith taught me to tear the paper off the crayon and make a beautiful picture anyway.

Somebody who was really good at this was a fellow named Paul. He wasn't particularly handsome. As a speaker, he was so naturally gifted and dynamic that one night part of his audience went to sleep and fell out the window. He was always getting beaten up or shipwrecked or run out of town.

But in the midst of all this adversity, he wrote a letter to a group of people in Rome who weren't exactly living in the Ritz themselves. He said, "For we know that all things work together for the good of those who love God and are called according to His purpose."

The Lesson of
KNOWING IN PART

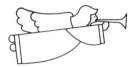

LIKE CIVILIZATIONS and countries and even families, Sunday Schools have histories. Sometimes the history of a Sunday School is written down, like the history of a country. And sometimes, like the history of a country, the history of a Sunday School contains the detailed accounts of wars and civil wars.

But Sunday Schools also have unwritten histories. Usually, the stuff of the unwritten histories is of the mishap variety—the accounts of people doing and saying the strangest things. These gather through generations and become part of the legend of the place. Most of these events are factual, real happenings to real people, but once they are inducted into the legendary hall of honor and go through frequent repeatings, the real facts may be revised, edited, and embellished in the name of good storytelling.

The following story is a part of the legend of the Sunday School of my childhood. Although the story is said to have happened even before I was born, I have heard it repeated so often that I now have a vivid memory of all the details as surely as if I had been there myself.

Charles Ray Lambert didn't come to Sunday School much. For one thing, he lived way out on the edge of the valley; and for another, he really didn't seem all that interested. Charles Ray didn't come enough to learn the etiquette of the place. He even wore his Everyday Shoes. When he did come, the teachers acted really excited to see him, but most of the other children just seemed to ignore him.

One day when Charles Ray was there, Mrs. Murphy, who was theologically committed to the principle of biblical memorization, assigned the class the task of learning her favorite passage, Psalm 23. Everybody was to work on it all week and next Sunday there would be a time for us to recite.

Well, on the next Sunday, Mrs. Murphy could tell that no one was familiar enough with the entire passage to risk it alone, so she had the class recite together. That way, individual students could hide in places of limited knowledge and she could still tell where the trouble spots were when the unison speech dimmed from vigorous clarity to quiet mumbling.

But those moments followed a pattern. The recitation smacked of confidence in the beginning, faded some during that middle part about the table and head, and picked up steam again for the finale.

When it was over, the class stood in satisfaction of what they had accomplished, but Jimmy Joe White, who was standing next to Charles Ray, asked loudly, "What did you say?"

Charles Ray answered in a defensive tone, "I said it." Of course, most of the students doubted this. They doubted that Charles Ray had even studied Psalm 23. In fact, most of them doubted that Charles Ray even had a Bible, although he said he did, a big white Bible with red letters and everything, but too big to carry to Sunday School.

"Say it for us, Charles," they all insisted. "Say that last part for us."

And Charles bowed his head and repeated what he thought he had heard. "And surely, good Mrs. Murphy will follow me all the days of my life."

That moment is part of the unwritten history of our Sunday School. The name of Charles Ray Lambert lives from generation to generation, and people young enough to be his grandchildren still tell the story and laugh heartily.

Everybody loves that story, except maybe Charles Ray. He never came back to Sunday School after that day in the limelight and he left the community when he was sixteen, never to return.

I can understand his plight and I'm not sure he needed to be all that embarrassed. For Charles Ray spoke for many of us, maybe most of us, that morning years ago, when he got enough courage to repeat for the public what he thought he had heard.

How often we hear only in part! How often we know only in part! How often, like Charles Ray, we send the concept from our eyes or ears to our brain in some sort of fog and haze, thinking all the time that we know the truth clearly.

One day, Jesus taught a great lesson about the promise of His Father's mansion and the joy of living there forever. But Thomas didn't get it. He couldn't comprehend and needed more explanation. So Jesus answered in words that made perfect sense to some, "I am the way, the truth, and the light."

But Thomas' later actions after the crucifixion and resurrection indicated that he didn't get that either. He was still in a fog when he came one day and demanded to touch the nail holes and inspect the damage.

Through thirty-seven years of learning what it means to live with Jesus within me, I have come to believe that much of Christian growth is this business of examining and rethinking basic ideas. How often I pick up my Bible to have it flop open to some familiar spot. How often I say, "I've already read these words at least a thousand times. I even have them memorized and can say them by heart." But how often I read anyway to discover a truth I have never seen before and then realize that all these years I have been reciting something that sounds like, "And surely good Mrs. Murphy shall follow me all the days of my life."

After we have finished laughing at the legend, perhaps we should bow our heads and ponder the lesson that Charles Ray Lambert taught us that day.

The Lesson of
SHORT PRAYERS

THOSE "OLOGISTS" who stay up late at night to ponder why humans act the way they do should spend some time studying why certain people get called upon most often to pray in church services.

When we were in the Kids Sunday School World, we had two out-loud prayers.

In the "huddled masses" meeting just before we broke away and ran off to our classes, we were led in prayer by either Mrs. Henderson or Mrs. Smith.

Mrs. Henderson was an old woman. Well, maybe she wasn't old all her life, but it seemed like she was.

Mrs. Henderson always taught the "younguns," those kids who couldn't read yet, and she knew a lot about God. When she led in prayer, she told God what she knew about Him. She knew a lot about the Bible, and when she led in prayer, she told God what the Bible said. She knew a lot about the world, and when she led in prayer, she told God what was going on in the world, as if it would come as a surprise to Him.

And Mrs. Henderson prayed on and on and on and on.

With our heads bowed and our eyes closed, we stood and stood and fought the anxiety to get to class. We always lost. For one thing, our feet began to hurt and our legs got tired. I'll never understand the reason for this. Boys can run and jump and kick clods and play for hours and not lose control of the calf muscles. But standing still for a five-minute prayer brings exquisite torture to the lower extremities.

After we stood on tired legs with our eyes closed for so long, we would begin to get dizzy. The world would spin, and we would lose our balance and begin to reel. And then we would bump into the kid next to us who was reeling some too. And he would push us, and we would push back. And about the time Mrs. Henderson was ready to tell God what was happening in the rest of the world, major conflict was erupting behind the curtain that turned our church into Sunday School rooms.

It wasn't just the idea of two kids wrestling that was so bad, but it was two kids wrestling with their heads bowed and eyes closed.

If these events are ever recorded in history, they will be called "The Wars of No Fair Peeking."

Mrs. Smith, who taught older kids, understood boys; and when she prayed, she prayed short. We didn't have time to get into tired legs or spinning worlds or wrestling matches. We just prayed and went to class.

It was during this period of my life that I grew to appreciate short prayers. As is often the case in theology, the reasons were practical at first, but later I searched the Scriptures until I found support.

When Paul was on his way to Damascus to do a little dirty work, he was stopped along the way by a light and a voice from heaven. From a prayerful posture of lying flat on the ground, he cried out to Jesus, "Who are You, Lord?"

The publican, with his head bowed out of humility and not duty, said, "God, have mercy on me, a sinner."

The leper kneeled in front of Christ and said, "Lord, if You are willing, You can make me clean."

Twenty-one words in all three, yet what else is there to say about the revelation of God, the power of God, and the will of God? It doesn't take so many words when you choose them well.

There are times in my life when I need the Mrs. Henderson style prayers, and I am glad for what she taught me years ago in that Sunday School opening assembly.

There are times when I need to kneel, bow my head, close my eyes to all distractions, and open my ego and essence to God. There are times when I need to lose track of minutes and even hours and give all the energy within me to the task of talking with God.

But there are times that I need the shorter version. I encounter events which require God's attention, but for which I do not have time for sufficient preparation or proper posture.

Just the other day, I was motoring along when two lanes blended into one, and some fellow in a Ford Taurus cut me off causing me to brake in a danger- ous way.

At that particular instant, I needed to call on the power of God, but if I had kneeled and bowed my head, I would have probably wiped out half a city block and a few dozen people.

Instead, with eyes wide open, I did a little para- phrase of the leper's request, "Lord, if You are will- ing, You can cleanse me of my vengeful thoughts," and He did. And then I pronounced another prayer. "Thank You for sending Mrs. Smith to teach me how to pray."

The Lesson of *LOOKING AHEAD*

MRS. FOSTER was my first grade teacher, and second grade, and third, and fourth. In our one-room schoolhouse, she taught all eight grades.

Because she was a typical teacher and we were typical students, we always knew what upset her. She didn't like it at all when we tripped or pushed during the recess basketball game, particularly when we were guarding her. She got upset when we didn't wipe our feet before coming back into the building after we had played Dare Base out in the mud. She yelled a lot if we left our half-eaten lunches in the cloakroom overnight and the mice got in. She didn't appreciate snakes in the schoolyard, and it always upset her for us to peek ahead in our books.

Sometimes we would try it when we were at the library. I just used the word "library" to make this sound more cultured and to make my schooling sound more credible. The library at our school was a steel cabinet full of books up at the front of the room.

Since the students in all eight grades used the same cabinet, Mrs. Foster usually supervised the time any one student would spend in the selection process.

But we would sometimes take advantage. If we thought she wasn't looking, we would slip out a book and browse. Usually the most appealing books for browsing were those volumes reserved for the people older than we were, unless, of course, we were in the eighth grade. Then we could browse in the first grade books.

But since this browsing time was guarded and precious, we would sneak our peeks at the last page. If the best part of a joke is the punch line, then surely the best part of a book is the last page. However, if Mrs. Foster caught us doing this, she would come by and thump the backs of our heads like they were ripe watermelons.

Then she would say, "Don't look ahead. You'll spoil the story." That's what she would always say — the same thing over and over again. With that kind of repetition, those seven words became more than just a reprimand, a reminder, or a lesson. They became a creed, a conscience; the rest of our lives we might peek ahead, but we would feel guilty about it with the voice of Mrs. Foster ringing in our ears and the memory of sharp pain banging on the backs of our heads.

But in Sunday School I confronted another lesson. It first happened on the day I gained the wonderful insight that the lesson leaflet they handed us every

Sunday morning was actually somehow related to that big black Bible Mrs. Murphy carried to class.

It was one of those significant "Ah ha!" moments of truth that come along periodically in our development and leave us wiser and more mature in their wake.

I am not even sure I know what triggered the insightful moment. I don't really recall any process of preparing the fertile field for learning unusual circumstances or specific teaching techniques.

At the time we were studying the life of King David. It seemed we had studied the life of David for the last six years, but it was probably more like three months.

On this day our leaflet was titled, "1 Kings 2:1-10, The Death of David," and in the last lines we read, "Then David rested with his fathers and was buried in the City of David."

Even at my young age, I knew that this would be the final chapter for old King David. Once you're buried, you don't get much written about you. I just knew that was the end of that story, and I went about the business of wondering who would be the hero of the next story.

Mrs. Murphy, also at a transition, closed her big black Bible and laid it on the empty front row chair just in front of me.

Being a kid afflicted with a normal amount of curiosity, I yielded to the urge to look in that book myself. (Years later, I have learned that yielding to curiosity is called research.)

I flipped open the book to a random spot and read "1 Kings 2—The Death of David." It was the same as the leaflet! I read on and saw the very same words we had been reading all morning. Finally, I came to the end of the story. ". . . and was buried in the City of David." Suddenly, it all made sense. The reason she had been reading the book was that it was the same as the lesson leaflet. Then I caught a grasp of the truth—the lesson leaflet had been taken from the Bible.

At that point, I got my taste of utter frustration. I had just learned something profound and deep and life-changing—something that deserved to be shouted from the mountaintop. But I was afraid to whisper it for fear that I was the only one in the whole class who hadn't known that fact in the first place.

But that wasn't the biggest shock. With a strong mental image of my schoolteacher causing me great feelings of guilt, I decided to peek ahead. When no one was watching, I would look up the next story and get a jump on the class for the weeks to come.

Rather than seeming too obvious, I grabbed a bundle of pages of the Bible the size that I could get between my thumb and forefinger, flipped over, and read, "Psalm 34—A Psalm of David."

"Wait a minute," I shouted to myself in the forced silence of my own guilt. "We've finished the story on David. Why is there more?" But there was more. That whole book was filled with the poems that were obviously written by David. I was fascinated with the possibility.

I couldn't wait to get to school the next morning. In those days, the first thing we did every Monday morning was to have a Sunday School debriefing. Mrs. Foster would move from seat to seat and ask each student for a full report. We would recite Bible verses, summarize themes, or explain some interesting piece of history or geography. This was a good way to make the transition from weekend to school week; we learned some Bible verses, but most importantly we learned the embarrassment of skipping Sunday School.

This particular Monday morning, I was prepared for the debriefing period. I had imagined how Mrs. Foster would look when I said it. She too would surely be surprised with my discovery.

So I explained what I had done, not leaving out a single detail. I explained how we studied the death of David. With only a hint of fear of correction, I told of peeking ahead. With enthusiasm, I revealed that there was more to the story and that maybe peeking ahead would not be wrong but even profitable.

Having delivered my story, I sat back waiting for Mrs. Foster to be as shocked as I was. But she wasn't. She only smiled and said, "Oh, yes, the Bible is different from any other book. It's even more exciting when you know how it's going to come out."

With that, she moved on to the kid behind me.

The Lesson of ROLLIE

ROLLIE WAS NOT a typical boy, but his story is typical because in every community and every Sunday School there is at least one person who finds the riches of God in a nontypical way.

From the very first days Rollie began to venture out into public, the whole community realized that he was different. He had an unusual amount of curiosity, more than is normal for a child his age, and unbridled curiosity is often labled something else and blamed for a plethora of strange behavior.

Perhaps his first moment of infamy came from his bout with the clock during his first grade year. Rollie didn't study much. Well, he didn't study the things in the book and on the board. Rollie studied things like Maxine's curls, the bolts in his desk, the cracks in the lump of coal before he put it in the stove, and mouse tracks in the cloakroom.

But these weren't the kinds of studies that thrill teachers, so Rollie got to stay in during recess a great deal of the time. I'm not sure I know what he did during those periods when he was in the building alone or sitting with Mrs. Foster, but I doubt that he studied what was in the book or on the board.

But I do know what he did one particular day. Mrs. Foster was outside playing basketball with the rest of us, and Rollie was in the room alone. That's when he decided to enter the fascinating world of clock repair, or at least clock investigation.

Mrs. Foster's clock was a part of the community legend because she had had it for so long. It was a large black Big Ben that sat up on top of the library cabinet and ticked loudly, particularly during those times when silence seemed to be in order. It sat perched way up out of easy reach because this clock was the official school timepiece, and we ate lunch and went home by the dictates of its ticking.

But that day during recess, Rollie, with his curiosity raging full speed, managed to get the clock down and was well into his third lesson of how the insides worked by the time the rest of us finished basketball and came back in to cipher some before the end of the day. Mrs. Foster was not pleased.

In literary language, this event was a foreshadowing, a sign of things to come. Rollie distinguished himself with such events and matters frequently.

In Sunday School, Rollie was active, and frequently, an active child is renamed The Terror. During opening exercises, he would get down on the floor and crawl around, untying people's shoes and investigating the streaks on the floor. During prayer time, Rollie was always in plain sight when we closed our eyes to start to pray, but he was nowhere to be seen when we opened our eyes, even during Mrs. Smith's prayers which were short.

During class time, Rollie was always the first one to claim a seat, but he never occupied it. He was always up, running around, going into other classes, and crawling on the floor.

In the wide open spaces outside the confines of school and Sunday School, Rollie was just as active, but he had more room to spread his behavior around. Rollie once threw a cat off the top of the barn to see if it would land on its feet. He got down on his hands and knees, played like a dog, and chased cars and chickens.

Once when he was a little older, he rigged up an old purse and made it look fat and prosperous and tied a big string on it. One night he put this purse on top of Beaver Creek Bridge, and when people in cars came rumbling by and saw that fat purse, they would screech to a halt and come running back to the promise of riches and prosperity. But just then Rollie would yank the purse off the bridge.

About the time he turned fourteen, Rollie got interested in motorcycles, and that's when the community gave him up as gone for good. He made his first scooter out of an old washer motor and spare parts, but after that he went on to bigger and better things. We lost track of him and didn't even know where he was much of his teen years.

Many years later, I found Rollie again and I know where he is and what he does. He works as a missionary repairman in a remote primitive village in the Amazon jungle, where his curiosity and talent with machinery make him a productive servant in the work of God. He can not only fix anything, but he can also build anything. He still has unlimited energy and works night and day. In other words, God is using him and his ability, all of it.

My story about Rollie isn't all that surprising or ironic. So why bother remembering and telling it? We need to recall it and think about it often, not for the Rollies of our generation, but for those of the next, for those young boys who take clocks apart and crawl on the floor during Sunday School, and for their teachers and parents. This is why people like Mrs. Smith and Mrs. Murphy and Mrs. Henderson get up an hour or two earlier every Sunday for twenty-five years, just to talk a bunch of children into such things as learning the books of the Bible in order and singing "Everyday with Jesus is sweeter than the day before."

Even though Rollie spent his time crawling on the floor and disappearing when our eyes were closed in prayer, and even though it didn't seem that he was hearing all that much at the time, I wonder how it would have all come out if Rollie had not been there at all — if there had been no Mrs. Smith who led the singing or Mrs. Murphy who taught about David. Would God now have a servant working on machinery in the Amazon jungle?

Actually, Rollie is not too different from the rest of us. Every one of us is our own Rollie story in a special kind of way. We are the purpose of the energies and the efforts and expenses called Sunday School, but we are more than that. We are also the living examples of the biggest lesson of all, because Sunday School is about the power of Jesus to change people.

We sang a little song about Zaccheus, that wee little man who climbed up into the tree. Jesus changed him. He kept what was good, whacked off what was bad, and turned him into an effective servant.

We read about Peter who denied Christ at His neediest moment. But Jesus changed Him. He kept what was good, whacked off what was bad, and turned him into an effective servant.

Now we study about Rollie and ourselves. Jesus can change us. He can keep what is good, whack off what is bad, and turn us into effective servants.

That's what Sunday School is about.

The Lesson of
THE DINNER TABLES

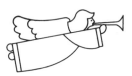

SOME LESSONS IN LIFE are easy to master. One fact mastered, one trial with correction, and we have a new habit. On the other hand, some lessons are difficult to learn.

Some lessons in life are probably not worth learning. Knowing where the Horse Latitudes are and how they got their name would be advantageous if you happened to get that question in a trivia game; but otherwise, it's just an interesting fact, unless, of course, you're a sailor. On the other hand, some lessons are absolutely valuable to living a worthwhile existence.

The lesson for today is of the second kind on both counts. Not only is it difficult to learn but it is absolutely one of the most important lessons I have ever encountered. After a series of trials and failures, I still wasn't any closer to mastering this seemingly simple concept, until one day in Sunday School class Mrs. Murphy made it all clear for me.

Mine was the last generation of our little church

to experience that evangelism strategy called "preaching all day and dinner on the grounds." I think it should be revived.

Several churches would join together and flock to one location. Services would begin about 9 A.M. and go almost until the evening milking time.

Ministers and musicians of every shape and style would expound and deliver and clarify and urge and hold forth, and our souls would be lifted.

But the most memorable part of the day was dinner. With our appetites sharpened by sitting through three sermons, four special music numbers, and hearty congregational singing, we rushed outside on the final "Amen" just to behold the sight.

Tables made out of doors lying across sawhorses seemed to stretch for about three city blocks, and those tables were loaded down with food, but more than just food.

Every human has a "tour de force," and the dishes on those makeshift tables stood as representations of the very finest that every cook in the valley had to offer. This was food at its best, good enough not only to eat, but to autograph. If you picked up any single dish and inspected the bottom, you could find the signature of the author affixed there with cellophane tape.

Although the food had been created by artists, it had been arranged on the table by behavioral scientists, people who understood human appetites and foibles. From the first time I ever attended one of those functions, I knew that salads always came first.

Now that I have grown older and understand how scientists work, I even know the reason.

I would tell myself as I started through the food line, "Don't fall victim to this plot. Use discretion. Control your greed." And I started taking a spoonful of this salad and a spoonful of that just to be polite, and maybe a couple of spoonfuls of this particular one because it was my favorite.

But, alas, all too quickly I discovered the finite limits of paper plates. And by the time I had reached the beans and vegetable casseroles, still a good forty feet away from the fried chicken, and sixty feet away from Mrs. Roush's currant pie, I had gone beyond the boundaries of aesthetic food arrangement.

I attended those functions for four years before I even got to taste meat. All the while, I thought it was just my problem. I had no idea that other people, particularly adults who are supposed to be mannerly and disciplined, had the same frustrations.

But one day in class, Mrs. Murphy made herself vulnerable. Good teachers do that occasionally.

We were studying the fourth chapter of Matthew, and old Satan was making it rough on Jesus. First Satan came with food and then with power and finally with wealth. Jesus resisted, and we boys, individually and collectively, were impressed.

"Wow, that's neat," we said, thinking that food, power, and wealth included just about everything that could ever be valuable in life. "He must be strong."

"Yes," she told us, and then she told us something

else which I pray that I never forget. "Jesus is more powerful than Satan."

"How powerful is He?" we asked in unison, with images from Captain Marvel comics dancing in our minds.

She paused for a moment, as teachers sometimes do when they confront an unexpected question and have to stall for time and answer. But frightened by the silence, she blurted, almost in embarrassment, what seemed to be the first thing in her mind. "He is so powerful that He could walk right by the salad table."

I knew what she meant!

The Lesson of
THE LOSER

LET'S START this lesson with a quiz. What's the name of the Bible story about the death of a giant?

I guess that you answered the way I always answered that question, until the Sunday Mrs. Parish came to teach our class.

It was during the flu epidemic, and Mrs. Murphy, the regular teacher, was home sick. Mrs. Smith, the superintendent of the children's division, who substituted at times like these, was out of town tending to her mother who had fallen and broken her hip.

That left the possibility of eight boys caged up in a small room with no supervision. I'm sure that prospect struck terror into the hearts of all those responsible for order in church.

That's when Mrs. Parish was recruited. "Recruited" is an euphemism, an understatement, a gentle way to describe what really happened. In other words, Mrs. Parish was accosted, forced, bribed, and manipulated, and yet, she still managed to smile when she entered the room armed with only a lesson leaflet and the promise that she wouldn't have to do this next week.

The first rule of teaching a class of boys is also the first rule of breaking a colt: "Don't let them see your fear." Mrs. Parish broke the first rule during the opening prayer, and we all knew that this would be a day to remember.

Next she began the lesson with a simple introduction. "Today we will study the story of Goliath and David."

With that blunder, almost everyone in class erupted in the kind of vigorous laughter that boys frequently use to point out adult mistakes. As young as we were, we still knew that the proper title of that battle story is "David and Goliath." No one had ever said it or heard it said or even thought about it as "Goliath and David."

Only I didn't laugh. It wasn't that I was more sensitive than the others. I just didn't get it as quickly. I had to ponder the situation and then have someone explain it to me before I could catch the humor.

So I just sat there and thought about what she had said for a few seconds. But I still didn't laugh, even after thinking about it. I was too intrigued with this new idea. It's one that deserves some attention.

In all my years of envisioning this story, of playing it out in vivid detail through the wonder of my mind's pictures, I had always seen it unfold through David's thoughts and eyes—his pleading to go to battle, struggling against the oversized armor, choosing the right stones, firing the missile, and watching the conquered giant fall in front of him.

But Mrs. Parish, with her trembling slip of tongue, gave my imagining a whole new dimension. There are two characters here—two minds, two sets of eyes, two plans of action. When we ignore Goliath's view in this story, we miss a very important point. From David we learn the lesson of the winner, but from Goliath we learn the lesson of the loser. And that lesson is too important to overlook.

For all we know, Goliath might have been a nice person underneath all his tough-guy exterior. He might have been a loving husband and father. We do know that he was a willing soldier ready to stand up for his leader and army. Of course, he probably didn't believe he was really risking all that much at the time.

But regardless of the kind of person he was, Goliath made one fatal error: he dared to stand up against God. That's the lesson we learn from the loser. Regardless of how tough we think we are, we can't stand up against God.

There have been those who have tried it, and we have accounts of the consequences. Pharaoh tried it, and Jonah, and Herod, and Ananias, and Goliath.

It would seem that from all this evidence that we would somehow manage to master this concept, but I am not sure I've learned it yet in its fullness.

In an attempt at justification, perhaps I could engage in a deep theological debate about what God wants from me, what His will is, and what the Bible really means, especially in its confusing parts.

But that's a smoke screen. When I finally come around to being honest with myself, I have to confess that I'm not even living out those parts of the Bible that are perfectly clear.

But I do have some help. Every time my memory wanders back to Sunday School days, and I remember Mrs. Parish's contribution to my moral development, I take a peek through Goliath's eyes and see that one stone coming straight for my head. And then I understand that it's always foolhardy to stand up against God.

 # The Lesson of
A MAN'S TEARS

"REAL MEN don't eat food that begins with the letter Q," the scholars of real men tell us. In fact, those scholars give us a whole list of don'ts for real men.

But at the top of this list of awesome don'ts that separate the macho from the meek, the weighty from the wimps, is the consistent code, "Real men don't cry."

That's the first law of the street. We begin to learn it about the same time we begin to eat with a spoon, and we have the lesson superimposed on our faces and personalities with the frequent repetition required of all good education.

At the height of his teasing, the bully taunts us, "What are you going to do? Cry?" as if crying would be the greatest imaginable display of human weakness.

When the ball hits us during the backyard game and we turn into patches of purple welts, we are constantly being reminded of the code. "Spit on it and play," we are told. "Whatever you do, don't cry."

Even mothers contribute to the cause. During the process of growing up, which for most of us lasts a lifetime, there come those moments when the logical response is just to sit and cry.

One of the fish in the tank dies. Our best friend can't come over, and everybody else doesn't want to come over either. The homework is too hard. When we get to grow the beans in a cup in class, ours are the puniest ones. The Cardinals lose a game.

Mother's function at these moments of tragedy is to come, wipe the tears away with the cleanest corner of her apron, and say, "Now you mustn't cry. Crying won't make it any better."

And from this, we learn early and know forever that real men don't cry.

David was a real man. We learned that in Sunday School once. In fact, we learned that in Sunday School one whole quarter.

We knew that quarter was going to be special the moment we saw the new Sunday School book. On the front cover was the picture of this gigantic man dressed in full armor, swinging a spiky ball around his head and sneering ferociously at this innocent looking boy standing in front of him holding a home-made slingshot. The picture itself told the story of valor, preparedness, innocence, and the unreasonableness of faith. Who could resist such an appeal?

The lessons inside only accented the theme. David was indeed a real man. He ate the right foods, he camped out in the wilderness, he was loyal to his friends, and he fought the enemy in the face of great odds.

In short, David became my hero. He was the kind of man I wished I could be. I think that's what having a hero means to all of us. In those places in our hearts where God is the only outsider allowed to visit, we wish we were the hero.

Most of us tell ourselves that we actually wish for the circumstances of heroism. We dream of that moment when we face the sneering, armed giant and attack with nothing but initiative and a smooth rock. We dream on of applause and accolades and honor that would surely come to us—if only we had the opportunity.

But the truth is, it isn't just opportunity that we lack. When the giant comes—and there are more giants in life than we often recognize—most of us are probably lurking way back in the foxholes somewhere sniveling with the rest of Saul's army.

But David was a real man. He stepped forward and fought the giant.

One day, Mrs. Murphy started the lesson by writing on the board in big letters, FRIENDSHIP, and we spent the whole hour imagining David and Jonathan running around the wilderness, hiding from Saul, sharing secrets and being buddies.

That's the stuff of real men too—having real buddies. Real men have buddies who require sneaking and thigh-slapping and loyalty.

But just about the time the bell was to ring, signaling the end of intentional learning, the beginning of socially inspired incidental learning, and peace to Mrs. Murphy, we hurried through those last few verses, crowding everything in to avoid the cardinal sin of omitting something important enough to be published in the quarterly.

It was Jerry Hill's time to read and he read fast like he was in a game of Hot Potato and didn't want to be "It" when the bell rang.

"After the boy had gone, David got up from the south side of the stone and bowed down before Jonathan three times with his face to the ground. Then they kissed each other and wept together—but David wept the most," he panted vocally at the end, proud that he had made it all the way through.

But even in the rush of the singsong reading, and the shuffling of a class of boys gathering their possessions, and the continued activity of such distractions, at the two-minute warning, I caught those last words, "But David wept the most."

Those words stabbed into my being with the cold piercing sharpness of a frozen knife. I wanted to cry out. I wanted commentary, explanation, or at least solace.

But the bell rang, and I lost not only teaching but companionship. I sat back down in the classroom all alone, and stared at that one word staring back at me from the board, FRIENDSHIP. And I thought and I thought. I thought until my brother came to find me and chide me for making him late to worship service again.

He stood at the door and rebuked. But I had to know the meaning of all this, and my brother was infinitely wise, being five years older than I.

I asked, "Do real men cry?"

"Of course not, Dummy," he answered with sibling cordiality, "but I'm going to make you cry if you don't come on."

"Was David a real man?" I asked again quietly.

"Sure! He whipped Goliath. Hurry up," he spoke from wisdom.

"But David wept the most?" The words came from and through the heart and mouth in such a way that the sentence became an interrogative instead of declarative. "How do you explain that?"

"There is a difference between weeping and crying," my brother said, just before he grabbed my ear and led me away.

I heard and I followed, and I thought about what he said, but I still think he's wrong.

The Lesson of
THE FIRST AND LAST

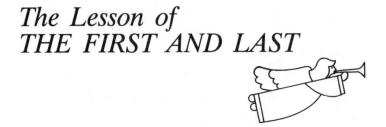

SOME BIBLE LESSONS are straightforward and blunt. Some Bible lessons are reminding and gentle. Some Bible lessons are refreshing and inspiring. And some Bible lessons are just plain tough. Not only are they difficult to apply, but just about the time you think you are beginning to know what the lesson has to say to the way you live, you sort of start wishing the Bible didn't say that at all.

Personally, I have always had trouble with Christ's promise or admonition – I can't really tell which – that the first shall be last and the last shall be first. I have heard the preachers exhort; I have read the commentaries; and I have even heard the televangelists proclaim. But I must confess that I'm still not really sure I understand all of what I am supposed to make with that piece of truth.

Nevertheless, I do have an illustration. In our Sunday School, we had two very different families – the Smiths and the Hendersons. The Smiths were always the first ones there. I am not sure I know how early they came because they had already arrived, turned up the heat, pulled the thistles away from the doors, settled in, dusted the piano, and drawn pictures on the chalkboard by the time anyone else got there. This wasn't just once; they did it every Sunday that I can remember. When my memory returns to boyhood and the joy of Sunday School, the first memory of all is walking into the building and being greeted by the Smiths. Because they got there first, they had their choice of all the seats in the house, so each one sat in the very same seat every Sunday with a sense of ownership.

The Smiths knew this about themselves and wore their early arrival like a badge of honor. It was their contribution to the Sunday School and to its legend. I think that if some other family had ventured out as early as the Smiths did, they would have probably stopped along the road somewhere just so the Smiths could keep their streak in tact.

On the other hand, we had the Hendersons. Just as the Smiths were always first, the Hendersons were always the last to arrive. They would come straggling in halfway through the song service, struggling with buttoning their shirts and tying their Sunday School Shoes. Mrs. Smith would occasionally even change the order of service so that we would pray after the Hendersons got there. Since the Hendersons were always late, they always had to take the last vacant seats. My memories of Sunday School include those images of the Hendersons tromping past seated people to get to vacant chairs.

The Hendersons knew this about themselves and wore their late arrival like a badge of honor.

The Smiths lived way back on the other side of the big hills, and were the only family that came from beyond those hills. In fact, the Smiths lived farther away than any other family, and the roads were bad out there.

The Hendersons lived next to the church. In fact, their yard butted up against the church lawn, and they had a path worn where they cut through every Sunday—not more than a hundred feet away by the shortcut.

I don't know how this applies to what Jesus taught us, but I do enjoy remembering it, and I think there may be a subtle message about human nature and even the Christian journey. Sometimes, the people with the farthest to go get there first.

The Lesson of
THE MEMORABLE PART

THE BIG EVENT each year was Sunday School Rally Day. This is the day we gave the whole Sunday service to things like teacher recognition and promotions and a big program. Rally Day drew the biggest attendance of the year. Maybe people came because all the children had a speaking part. On the other hand, maybe they came because the preacher didn't have much of a speaking part.

The purpose of the day seemed to be to showcase talent and training. We recited the Bible verses we had learned, sang the songs we had prepared just for the event, gave an exhibition Sword Drill, and staged a play with memorized lines and everything.

The play was a big deal, and the assignment of parts was a major test of social science insight and theatrically educated hunches. Our Sunday School world was divided into two kinds of people — those who wanted a part in the play and weren't ashamed to admit it, and those who wanted a part in the play but were too embarrassed to show it. Mrs. Smith, who assigned the parts, seemed to understand that. Sometimes she would give the biggest part to the person who protested the most about even being in "a sissy old play" much less starring in it. But this was always the person who beamed the most when we took the curtain call.

One year we staged the Parable of the Prodigal Son. Mrs. Smith wrote the play herself, so she understood it well, and she understood us too. Since there were two party scenes, she had minor parts for almost everybody, and she assigned those first.

The rest stood around waiting with great anticipation and feigned apprehension. Some kids had even read ahead and knew what the choice parts were. Roger Mahoney was given the part of the older brother because, as Mrs. Smith explained, he had the personality for it. And since Roger hadn't read ahead, he thought that was a compliment. Then Mrs. Smith assigned the younger brother and even the father to the logical choices, and we all nodded agreement with her expertise.

And finally everybody had a part, except Dennis Jarvis, the chubby kid in our class. He might have been a nice person deep down inside, but nobody would ever know that because everybody picked on him so much that he had to be ornery in self-defense. Dennis didn't really stutter, but he talked so fast that he had to back up once in a while to get in the syllables he had left out the first time through.

And when he didn't have a part, we wondered if maybe Mrs. Smith had forgotten, but we wondered only a moment. In her typical ability to make the simple sound important, Mrs. Smith explained that she had saved the best part of all for Dennis. He would play the role of the fattened calf. Even though we wanted to laugh, we didn't until Dennis laughed. He enjoyed the role.

On Sunday School Rally Day, Dennis played his role to the maximum. He made a costume by putting a paper bag over his head and wearing a set of construction paper horns. He came on stage walking on all fours, and he bellowed and stomped just like a real calf. And the congregation laughed their appreciation.

When it was all over and we took the curtain call, Dennis got the biggest and wildest applause, even bigger than Roger Mahoney got for playing the older brother, and he had the personality for the part.

I had the opportunity to visit my old home church a couple of years ago. Although it had been forty years, the place looked just the same, only smaller, and the memories wiped forty years of wrinkles off my face and heart just for a moment.

That day I met an older man who would have been in the audience when we portrayed the story of the Prodigal Son on that Sunday School Rally Day.

He helped me remember, and his recalling powers were good, except that he kept running generations together and told me about people who were at least seven years older or seven years younger than I, as if they were my peer group.

Finally, there came a time in the conversation

when it seemed appropriate to ask about Dennis Jarvis. I realized there was a risk involved since Dennis was not particularly the memorable type. But as soon as I breathed his name, the older gent grinned a beacon of recognition and exclaimed in full appreciation, "Oh, you mean the kid who played the fattened calf?"

Throughout Hollywood, throughout Broadway, throughout all of India, there are men and women who make their living at acting who could only wish for what Dennis accomplished on that makeshift stage while wearing a paper sack over his head. He created a role that would live in the memories and hearts of those who saw him.

To make this a better story, I would tell you that Dennis is now a successful business executive. But the man I was talking with didn't know where Dennis was. And neither do I. But that doesn't matter. Dennis still had his moment of greatness.

The Lesson of
THE TALENTS

IN SUNDAY SCHOOL I learned the lesson of the talents. Maybe I should say I learned the lessons of the talents because, as is often the case, there are at least two lessons here. There is the lesson they teach you in class and the lesson you learn just hanging around paying attention.

The lesson we learned in class was noteworthy enough. We actually covered this section of the Gospel of Matthew during Mrs. Murphy's flannelgraph story.

Dedicated teacher that she was, she went so far as to make herself an apron covered with the flannelgraph stickum stuff so that as the lesson unfolded she could slap those scenes up on her chest with both hands. It was almost as good as the Saturday afternoon Western down at the Rialto Movie House.

On the morning of the lessons of the talents, the scenes and images manipulated by her dextrous fingers literally flew by and stuck permanently in our impressionable minds made even more impressionable through the use of the sense of seeing as well as hearing.

First we learned all about the guy with five talents, about his busyness and hard work and business acumen. But most of all, we learned about happiness. Mrs. Murphy didn't mention it because she didn't have to. It was presented in vivid color across her chest. That man smiled when he received the talents. He smiled as he worked, and everybody smiled during the reunion when his master came back.

The story was about the same for the fellow with two talents; but when we saw the man with only one talent, the whole tone changed. From the beginning, you could see that this was a person afraid. He looked sad while he received the talent; but more than sad, he seemed to be filled with feelings of suspicion. He had that look about him that Roger Brady had the day he brought Life Savers to Sunday School and tried to eat them without being caught by the teachers, or by other kids who would have demanded that he share.

The reunion for the one-talent man was especially sad. The master was harsh and the man was dejected and went off and cowered in a corner.

That's the story we saw in class, and its lesson was just as powerful. We learned that we should all use our talents regardless of what they were. We also learned that some of us had been given five talents, some had been given two talents and some of us had only one.

As dutiful children in Sunday School, we all sat

and agreed with that principle because we already knew who among us were cute, who could sing, who could play ball, and who got the biggest part in the Rally Day program. We knew about the rationing of talents.

But I learned another lesson of talents by watching the Sunday School administration. Mrs. Smith was the person in charge of the little kids' section, and she was good. In fact, she was about the best-liked person in all of the church.

Because of that, they made her Superintendent over the whole Sunday School. After that, nobody liked her much. The change in status came from her position and not from her personality.

As best as I can tell, the Sunday School Superintendent's biggest job is to find somebody to act as teacher in every class. As best as I can tell, there are two kinds of teaching appointments. There are lifetime appointments and panic appointments. In other words, there are those teachers who come from the womb with a Scripture Press Quarterly in one hand and a box of broken crayons in the other. These are the Lifers. They are born to teach.

On the other hand, there are those teachers who are pressed into the corps from the panic caused by the thought of half-crazed junior high youth running loose in a small room with no adult supervision. They are forced into teaching because of this inherent panic, and they respond with the same kind of emotion.

As best as I can tell, the secret to good Sunday

School management is to keep the Lifers and the Panickers apart. The Lifers are always telling us of things like dedication and devotion. "I always begin my lesson preparation on Sunday afternoon a full week ahead," they explain to the rest of us. "That way, I can have the whole week to search the commentaries, brush up on the Greek verbs, and create my own flannelgraph materials."

Do you have any idea what that kind of talk does to a person already pressing against multiple layers of panic and wondering if there is enough time on Saturday night to scan a text?

Well, this is the problem Superintendent Smith confronted, and it helped me understand how we all feel about the Parable of the Talents—not how we feel theologically but practically. Nothing brings out my appreciation of that text as effectively as asking a reluctant prospect to teach the sixth grade boys.

Except for those Lifers, most folks don't really believe they have more than one talent, and they repel all invitations to serve, not because they are lazy, but because they are trying to be realistic. And they may be close to accurate.

As best as I can tell, most of us do expect our teachers to have the encouraging ability of a Barnabas, the exegetical skill of a Paul, the storytelling gift of a Nathan, the musical talent of a David, and the work ethic of a Martha. And one-talented people need not apply.

That's the lesson I learned from Mrs. Smith.

The Lesson of
FINGER LICKING

I ALWAYS LIKED the game of Sword Drill because it reminded me of basketball. It was fast-paced, and the action came in spurts sprinkled throughout large blocks of anticipation time. Success depended on an unusual combination of skill and accident, and to the uneducated eye, it all looked disorganized, just like basketball.

But I liked Sword Drill better than basketball because I was good at Sword Drill. I was almost the best. Actually, I was second best. The only person I couldn't beat was Mary Alice Bickford, and that was disheartening. I dreaded going up against her. My stomach would knot up, and I would make my head hurt from squinting my eyes so I could concentrate on the text and my cognitive map of the Bible as I waited for Mrs. Smith to say, "All ready.... Charge!"

At that command, I would tear into my Bible as fast as I could, working my fingers through the pages and flipping and turning, and just as I was no more than two chapters away, Mary Alice would start to read, and I was beat again.

It wasn't just a matter of getting beat that was so painful, but it was getting beat by Mary Alice. When she won, she didn't gloat, and that made it bad. People are always saying how they love a gracious winner; but frankly, I don't much appreciate a gracious winner when the person they beat to get there is me.

The bad thing about Mary Alice's attitude is that she didn't gloat, she didn't boast, and she didn't act modest either. She just stood there about as unemotional as a person ought to be after she has just knocked off the whole children's Sunday School department for Sword Drill Championship of the Western World. The thing that bothered me most was she didn't even look surprised that she had beat me. She just looked as if this was what she intended to do in the first place.

I have been around sports enough to know that at the times in your life when you are only second best, and really want to be first best, you have two options. You can learn to cheat or you can practice. I opted for the second option. I practiced. I worked hard. I did finger exercises. I carried a tennis ball in my pocket and squeezed it to build up wrist muscles. I sat up late at night and wrote the books of the Bible in order. Then when I had mastered that, I practiced holding entire books in my right hand so that I would recognize just what the Book of Proverbs felt like between the finger and the thumb.

I even went so far as to add a few strategic dog-ears at the beginning of such sections as the minor prophets.

In short, I was prepared for the next Sword Drill battle. Again, I drew Mary Alice, and because this was the championship set, we had to go the best three out of five rounds. The first command was Romans 8:29, and I was only two verses away when Mary Alice began to read, and then she stood there looking not surprised.

Down but not out, I stuck a Life Saver in my mouth for the quick energy I would need for the second round. This time it was Exodus 48:2, and I was right there. I even had my finger on the very verse itself, and Mary Alice started to read.

Down the opening two, I lost all hope. I didn't tell anybody, and I tried to look confident, but I was lying. I knew I wasn't going to win. I knew that I would have to spend the rest of my life being second best. When Mrs. Smith gave the text and she called the charge, I didn't even open my Bible. Instead, I turned to watch Mary Alice. And that's when I learned her secret. She licked her fingers. Just when Mrs. Smith cried, "Charge," Mary Alice licked her fingers.

That's what I learned from Sunday School Sword Drill and Mary Alice Bickford. And it is one of the most important lessons I mastered during those growing years.

I hear you scoff. "How can such a thing as learning to lick your fingers before you flip through the

Bible be so consequential?" you ask.

But this lesson has immediate application. Many a time on Sunday morning, this little piece of simple knowledge has turned a potentially confusing situation into a significant spiritual experience.

For one thing, during the morning worship service, I always sit as far away from the preacher as I can get. This practice has some obvious advantages, but there is one distinct disadvantage. It takes sound a lot longer to travel back to where I am. How often the preacher enjoys giving the Scripture text in crescendo. He begins, "Today, we are going to read about times like now. Today, we will read words that are just as relevant as they were when they were written thousands of years ago. Today, we will read of a man who speaks the word of God." Meanwhile, the pitch and pace are rising, and I sit with the Bible poised and the anticipation of a Sword Drill charge to follow. Then he says, "Today, we will read from (long pause) Obadiah chapter two." Then he breathes a short breath and starts to read, thinking that everybody in the congregation is following along word for word.

There is, of course, an important preaching principle applied here. Preachers are taught this in seminary, and even those who make bad grades master it well. The more obscure the passage, the less time you give the congregation to look for it.

But I am on top of this—with Sword Drill experience and my piece of knowledge. I just lick my fingers and get there.

But even beyond this, this little lesson has metaphorical application as well. How often we tell ourselves that a task is too tough for us. How often we begin to accept ourselves as second best. How often we talk ourselves out of trying. And all the time, the secret is as simple as licking your fingers. What a philosopher that Mary Alice Bickford was!

Just the other day, one of my bosses called me into his office. He had been away to an important seminar on people management and other such learned skills, and he wanted to practice his new lessons in an attempt to justify the money he had spent.

He moved out from behind his desk and sat just across from me looking me straight in the eyes. He unfolded his arms and uncrossed his legs and looked as if he were truly open to my suggestions.

He bent over and closed the distance between us, and in a tone that sounded as if he had a significant institutional secret which we had to protect with our lives, he said, "Cliff, there's a difference between working hard and working smart." He leaned back and took the posture and tone that said that he was satisfied with himself for having revealed that to me, and he said, "Do know what I mean?"

"Yes," I answered. "I think I do. It's like Mary Alice Bickford licking her fingers in Sword Drill."

I don't need the seminars. I've been to Sunday School.

The Lesson of JOHN 3:16

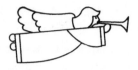

PROGRESS is more than jumping at whatever is new. It is also diligently clinging to what worked in the past.

Mrs. Murphy was a progressive teacher. She used flannelgraph before some of the others had even settled the question of whether it was theologically sound. She used a tape recorder even before there were cassettes. She made copies before mimeographs, when she had to print sheet by sheet with a rolling pin and a pan of jelly. And she gave us Life Savers for getting the answers right.

Yet, Mrs. Murphy clung diligently to what was sound in the past. In other words, she believed in Bible memorization. She not only believed in Bible memorization as a teaching tool, but she had even memorized major sections herself. That's how much she believed in it.

Every Sunday, she would start the class by standing in front of us and reciting some significant portion. But with Mrs. Murphy Bible memorization and recitation was different. Some people seem to memorize Scripture for the same reason that other people take cold showers. If they didn't do it, they wouldn't have anything else to brag about.

But during Mrs. Murphy's recital, we students got the idea that this was important for other reasons. With her it seemed significant, a crucial step in her spiritual walk; and even on those frequent occasions when we students didn't fully grasp all the content, we still listened in the kind of awed silence that children are trapped into involuntarily on those rare times when they are genuinely impressed.

In recent years when such things as children and Sunday Schools are being visited by calculator-carrying social scientists, the teaching/learning technique of Bible memorization has fallen on some rough times. Of course, I'm not much of a scientist but only a reminiscer, and I don't want to dispute their work. But I do enjoy remembering Mrs. Murphy recite, and I hope my granddaughter will someday enjoy the same kind of moment.

Mrs. Murphy not only memorized herself, but she turned us into memorizers as well. She made it an assignment, and we did it. I am not sure I remember why. There weren't any grades in Sunday School, so that wasn't a factor. We didn't have telephones, so she couldn't threaten to call our parents. Just getting one Life Saver a Sunday wasn't enough of a bribe to hold us to task during the whole week it took to memorize. Maybe we worked at our memorization because we liked the way Mrs. Murphy did it.

I shall never forget the Sunday we started. She introduced the class with a long recitation of a Psalm, and we listened as intently as if David himself were singing. Then she stopped and said, "Next week, it will be your turn," and we stared at each other in feigned fear.

"You will memorize one verse and recite it for the class next Sunday," she continued the assignment.

We responded with the standard protests that are required by the Laws of International Studentship anytime any assignment is given.

"We've never ever done this before."

"Does the other class have to do it?"

"Can we put it off a week?"

"This is dumb."

She stood her ground, and we surrendered easily, mostly because we knew it would be exciting.

But after she had persuaded us that we would do the assignment, we had to get a clarity in the directions. This is also required by the Laws of International Studentship.

"Does it have to be a whole verse?"

"Can it be more than one verse?"

"If we memorize two verses, can we use one for the Sunday after?"

"Can we memorize a verse from the New Testament?"

"Can we memorize a verse from the Old Testament?"

"Can we memorize a verse from the concordance?"

"What is a verse?"

Once we had exhausted the list of requisite questions, a sort of positive anxiousness fell on the room. It seemed that we all wanted to get into it. I told you that Mrs. Murphy was a progressive teacher.

That afternoon, while most of the family was napping, I borrowed my mom's Bible to begin preparation. At that time I didn't know much about what was in that rather austere looking black book. I had begun to read it once from the beginning, but I hadn't really made it out of the Garden of Eden yet. The only other thing I knew about it was those words and phrases that sort of hopped off the page while I was flipping through enroute to the beginning, and the most impressive one of those was something named Selah.

But this day was different. I would have to recite what I had learned, so I needed to search for the right verse. This was more than an exercise of personal memorization. This was also our introduction to Christian witnessing.

Some of my mom's Bible was printed in red; and being the strategist that I was, I reasoned that what was in red must be the most important. I would go for something in red. So I plopped the Bible down, and it sort of fell open to this particular spot as if it had a mind of its own. From my own personal experience and hearing other people talk, I think Bibles do this occasionally.

With my finger, I touched one of the red verses and read, "For God so loved the world that He gave

His only begotten Son that whosoever believeth in Him should not perish, but have everlasting life."

From that moment on, I have known what it is to discover gold. I didn't know all the words, and I had trouble pronouncing what I did know. But that didn't matter. I knew enough to recognize that this was truth. Here was what I needed to know. Here was soothing water for the burning from my boyish fears. I read it over and over and over. I began to memorize, and the task was easy. The words seemed to stick in my brain. In that one short session, I mastered the memorization.

But that wasn't enough. I practiced all week. I said it to the cows while I milked. I said it to the hogs as I poured slop first in the small trough and then in the big one. In class, I said it under my breath between the school work. "7 x 9 is 63 For God so loved the world 8 x 7 is 56 that He gave His only Son—that He gave His only begotten Son 6 x 7 is . . ."

After about two months of that, next Sunday came and brought with it my big opportunity.

The verse was so powerful and I could say it so well that I just knew that I would be an instant hit in the whole class.

When it came time to volunteer for reciting order, I thought about holding my hand up quickly like kids do when they demand to be first, but I realized that would be too obvious. Instead I hung in the background and waited until I was assigned fifth. That was a good spot. I would wait with that opossum look as if they were all better than I; then I would spring it on them right in the middle.

Bobby Lee Stockton was first, and after some required protests about position and posture (more Laws of International Studentship), he moved to the front, grinned a bit, and said, "For God so loved the world that He gave His only begotten Son, that whosoever believeth in Him should not perish, but have everlasting life." To make it even worse, he said it perfectly.

I was stunned. That Bible is full of verses, more than people can even count, so why did he pick that one? Besides, that verse had jumped out at me as if it were my very own. And now here was my verse in the mouth of somebody else. I was not only stunned, but I felt a little betrayed.

If I showed it, Mrs. Murphy either didn't notice or was gracious enough to act as if she didn't, so we went on to Roger Goodner who was second.

He stood, grinned, and said, "For God so loved the world that He gave His only begotten Son . . ."

To make a long story short (if it's not too late already), six of the eight had memorized John 3:16, and the other two had discovered the delight of "Jesus wept."

Now, you may think that this day was one of the blue letter disappointment days of my life. But no day is a disappointment if it has pleasant consequences, and this day has proven to be one of my great moments.

Of course, I learned shortly after that this whole thing was a put-up job. Those kids had all memorized John 3:16 for vacation Bible school the summer before, and they were just taking the easy way out.

But that still doesn't deter from the awesome and comprehensive content of the verse. In fact, it adds to it. Because of the sequence of events that day, I have learned something really important about John 3:16. It is my very own verse that God gave specially to me. But He also gave it to a lot of other people for their special verse too—Bobby Lee Stockton and Roger Goodner and that person who goes to football games and holds up the sign when the television cameras are focused on the end zone.

It belongs to each one of us specially, and to all of us specially. And that makes us a family.

Sometimes I get caught in those situations when I just can't get to my Bible for devotions that day. So I say John 3:16, refresh my soul, and remember practicing it to the cows.

Sometimes I try to pray, and my mouth spits out brain dust instead. So I say John 3:16, refresh my soul, and remember practicing it to the hogs.

Sometimes I become God's agent in inviting and welcoming new members into the family. So I say John 3:16, refresh my soul, and tell them the Sunday School story, partly to break the ice, and partly because I want them to memorize it too.

I think I know how Mrs. Murphy must have felt that day.

The Lesson of
THE NEW BOOK

I FEEL SORRY for people who don't go to Sunday School. That's one place where the Bible lesson refreshes us with promise and challenge, where the fellowship reminds us that we are not alone, and where the food at the carry-in dinner is memorable.

Those are the obvious good times, but there are some subtle good times that are just as delightful.

Personally, I look forward to the day we get new Sunday School books. Isn't this wonderful? For those regulars in Sunday School, we always have this big day of anticipation just ahead. It's like being a student and living in a state of expectancy until the last day of school. It's even better because it comes once every three months.

When I was a child and life had not yet become burdened with too many books, that day of the new Sunday School book was one of the major events of my life. Back then the volume was called the Quarterly, and it was more than a mere collection of lessons for the next three months. With a cover adorned with a picture appropriate for the season, the Quarterly was a symbol of progress—maybe not the progress of the species, but at least of the individual. The new Quarterly told us that the past was over and that there was an excitement on the road yet in front of us.

In our little Sunday School, Mrs. Smith was in charge of the distribution. The big moment came at the very conclusion of opening exercises. As the creed required, we would sing, listen to an introduction to the lesson, collect the birthday offering, and pray. Usually, upon pronouncement of the Amen, we would all make a mad dash to our own little corner room and fight for available chairs. But on the special day of the new Quarterly, we didn't break away. We stood in boy reverence—which is not to be confused with real reverence, and waited with boy patience—which is not to be confused with real patience, as Mrs. Smith moved among us, diligently and tenderly handing each person a new book which contained the joy and the hope of the next three months. It was a big moment, even for those who never studied; and it was always the kind of moment which made you glad that you came to Sunday School and made you especially happy that you had come this particular day.

That's the way it was during my boyhood days in the valley, and that's the way it still is for me. But getting a new book is more than just another Red Letter Day in our lives. There seems to be an important lesson here. On the other hand, maybe there isn't any lesson at all; but through my years as a teacher facing the charge of filling a full hour every Sunday morning with something valuable, I have learned to spot lessons even in those places where none exist.

Nevertheless, I would like to think I can find at least one lesson lurking in the ritual of getting new books, and that is the lesson of timing.

When we first get the new books, they literally glow with newness. They feel new. They smell new. The colors are brillant; the type is bold and read-able; and the pages lie flat.

But during three months of use, wear takes a toll. The colors in the pictures smudge. The type fades. Fingerprints cover essential concepts, and coffee stains blot out hundreds of years of Hebrew history. Those pages which aren't dog-eared curl up so that you either have to study the lesson with an iron on hand or bend your neck to read words on a curve.

Just as you think nothing else could go wrong, the staples back out and twenty-seven percent of the pages fly loose in your hand.

At least, that's the way my lesson book looks. I notice that other people in class have better pre-served models, but I just tell myself that they don't study as much as I do. Still, I have to wonder why they can answer more questions.

But there is always hope. On that very Sunday when you have to gather up the remains from all corners of the house and know that you can't go through this one more time, you get a new book and start all over. This is the excitement of timing.

About the time the old book completely disintegrates, we get a new one.

About the time our lap begins to spread, we get grandchildren to fill the extra space.

About the time we have so much arthritis in our hands that we can't floss, our teeth fall out.

About the time we lose all confidence in the human race, the harried woman in front of us with a whole cart of groceries steps aside and lets us go first through the checkout line.

When the time is right, Jesus will come again.

Now, I realize that there is a pretty huge theological chasm between the idea of worn-out lesson books and Christ's coming. Nevertheless, there seems to be a powerful underlying thought at work here.

God is in charge of the dimension of time. That's good to know. No, that's *great* to know. In one of his letters, Paul got so excited about that little piece of factual information that every time he thought about it, he would stop and say, "Now encourage one another." In other words, living our lives in constant and operational knowledge that God is in charge of time is about the most encouraging thought we can ever have.

Bookstores are filled with volumes which tell us how to think positively and behave as if we think positively. Maybe we just need to remember that God is in charge of time.

But remembering this is tough because it requires the practice of patience. We often talk of patience as if it is a good thing to have. We even pray for patience. But we pray impatiently.

When I was a teenager, I prayed for a pickup truck. In those days, a pickup truck was the symbol of manliness, rugged individualism, and freedom.

I didn't want just any pickup truck. I wanted a pickup truck with outside mirrors, a gun rack, and a big dog policing the back, riding along with his face in the wind.

I prayed vigorously. I prayed impatiently. After a while when I didn't get a pickup truck, I quit praying.

Thirty years later, after I had grown out of being a teenager and had matured into manhood, I got a pickup truck. But by this time, it was a symbol of service. I could help people move, help clean up garbage, and haul the tables around for the church social—just another reminder that God is in charge of timing.

Every three months, I enjoy getting my new Sunday School book. I like the way it feels in my hands. But I particularly enjoy remembering to pray for patience.

The Lesson of "AND LO"

CHRISTMAS AND SUNDAY SCHOOL go together. Like ham and eggs, bread and butter, and Mutt and Jeff, the words blend into one image and one memory. I'm not sure how people who didn't grow up in Sunday School celebrate the Christmas season, but they have to be missing something.

Without Sunday School, how would you even know that Christmas was coming, and that it was time to start building good will and anticipation?

For us, the harbinger, the first hint, was the assigning of parts. Some Sunday morning, before anyone quite expected it, Mrs. Smith would announce in opening exercises, "Today we must begin to work on the Christmas program."

Next she would distribute parts. From those handwritten sheets with our names at the top, we got the idea that Mrs. Smith had stayed awake way into the night for several nights just thinking about each one of us and what we could do special to help our whole church see Christ in Christmas.

Then she would call on the kid with part One, and he would read, "There were in the same country shepherds abiding in their fields, keeping watch over their flocks by night. And lo, the angel of the Lord came upon them, and the glory of the Lord shone round about them; and they were sore afraid." And with that the Christmas season officially began in our valley.

In later years as I have become more metropolitan in my outlook, living in a town with a traffic light, I have often been amused by the attempts of merchants to announce the Christmas season. They decorate their windows in red, string banners across main street, hire Santa Claus to do television commercials, stuff Sunday papers full of slick pages, and give out calendars.

But I have a better idea. I think it would be simpler and more definite if they could find some kid with boyish cracks in his voice and optimism in his volume to read over a giant loudspeaker, "There were in the same country, shepherds abiding in their fields." Then the world would know that at that instant we should begin the celebration.

To this day, Luke 2 is still a very special spot in my Bible. I don't read it casually or carelessly or too often. Even when I'm reading through the good doctor's Gospel from cover to cover, I skip that part, and wait until that particular day.

You know the day. It comes in July or August. It is that day when the problems rain down like hailstones and pelt you, making your ears and spirit sag.

But you see through the problems to a clear and reasonable solution and yet, no one else in the world can see the solution, and so you stand alone. That's what is called a bad day. In the bright sun, there is no light. In the heat, there is no warmth. In the land of promise, there is no hope. Then I read Luke 2: "There were in the same country shepherds abiding in their fields, keeping watch over their flock by night. And lo, the angel of the Lord came upon them." And Christmas comes to my soul again.

Luke 2 is more than a passage to be read. It is to be partaken by all the senses. It even has its own fragrance — the smell of cedar and cinnamon.

Even in the beginning for me, those words carried significance, but I must confess that I didn't understand them all. From the process of contextualization (I love that word), I figured out the meaning of "abiding" by myself. But for the life of me, I could not decipher the word "lo."

Rather than looking it up in the dictionary which would have been the simple way out, I consulted a sage. I asked my brother. Because he was five years older than I was, he was the living expert on every human matter.

One night during that time of year when we fought each other for covers and visions of chocolate covered cherries danced in our heads, I asked him, "What is lo?"

"What?"

"What is lo?"

"It's underneath," the man of wisdom explained.

"No, it isn't." I was impatient. "It's in the Bible."

"Where?" he said in tones that frustrated me that he wasn't thinking about this too.

"In the Christmas story," I told him. "And lo, the angel of the Lord came upon them."

"Oh, that. Lo is the sound the sheep make," he said rather nonchalantly and went off to sleep.

For the next five years, I spent the Christmas season being a little upset that nobody went "Lo, lo, lo" during the Nativity part of the Sunday School program.

Those Sunday School Christmas programs were major parts of our lives. They were even bigger than Rally Day programs. On Rally Day the people came from all over the community, and we had a big crowd. For the Christmas program, they not only came from all over the community but they brought their kinfolks from California and other exotic places from far-off distances, and we had a gigantic crowd, and cosmopolitan too.

Seeing it all in retrospect, which is an educational way to see it, I realize that those programs served a valuable function in our celebration of Christmas because they gave the whole season a sense of structure and purpose. We had to learn our parts. We had to overcome our fears of performing in public. We had to share ourselves. We had to give something of ourselves. Because of the Christmas program, we couldn't go into the season with hearts of selfishness and greed.

Perhaps it seems like a small gesture now, but

giving ourselves to the Christmas program was at least a form of giving. At one time in one generation, there were fourteen children in that little country church who performed in the programs and gave themselves in a small way.

Now thirty years later, each one is serving God, either as a leader in the church world or as a leader in a local church. Somewhere they learned something good.

Not only does Christmas have a definite beginning moment from the world of a Sunday School memory, but it has just as definite a conclusion point as well. Christmas is officially over when you eat the last pecan.

That image comes out of the second great feature of the Sunday School Christmas celebration—The Tradition of the Sack.

We didn't give away treats or toys or even bags. We gave sacks. At the conclusion of the Christmas program, after the final chorus of "Silent Night" and the bow-taking, and the grinning sheepishly among the feelings of "I knew I would be the star," we all sat down, and the men of the church came up and handed out "the sacks."

We lived for the sacks. This was one of the great anticipation points of the winter season. They were filled with all sorts of good things, an orange and an apple, chocolates, hard candy, orange candy slices, peanuts and pecans.

Things like the orange slices and chocolates went fast. The hard candy was put into storage to be savored on long winter nights when you had to do chores after dark. Since the peanuts required both hands and couldn't be eaten with gloves on, we saved those for the evenings when we were reading in our bedrooms.

But the pecans were the biggest challenge. They were almost seductively delicious, but eating them required singleness of purpose. We didn't have a nutcracker, so the only way to achieve the joy of the taste was to mash two of them together in our hands. It was a slow process, but worth the effort.

About two weeks later when the sack was only a dim recollection and good will was beginning to wane, we would be rummaging through the sofa cushions and would discover that one lone pecan that had been dropped in our haste when the sack was still full and our hearts were light.

Since we didn't have but one, we had nothing to mash it against, so we would bash it with our shoe and eat so slowly, making the memory last and last and last until once more some kid would stand up in Sunday School and read, "There were in the same country shepherds abiding in their fields keeping watch over their flocks by night. And lo, the angel of the Lord came upon them, and the glory of the Lord shone round about them; and they were sore afraid."

The Lesson of
THE FOUR COLORS

ONE MAJOR PROBLEM in the world is that we don't listen enough to little children. We jest about something called "out of the mouths of babes," and we all know a story or two about how a young person spoke some pertinent insight that set the situation straight. But most of the time, we dismiss what children say and do as just so much child's play. Once in awhile I realize how really shortsighted that is.

Not long ago I had to visit a school because the administration wanted to talk with me about their problems. There was unrest among the faculty. Funds were in short supply. Everywhere I go anymore, money seems to be one of the problems, and as I examine matters more closely, often it becomes The Problem. In addition to all these problems, in this school, parents were upset and were protesting various affairs and situations. And I was going to the school to work as a mediator. Needless to say, this didn't have the promise of being a wonderful afternoon.

As I walked across the playground on my way to the battleground, I passed by a group of young girls who were involved in a rather advanced stage of jump rope. This group of children was what some would call a rainbow coalition. It appeared that the only requirement of membership was to be rather accomplished at jumping.

Walking by as casually as I could so I wouldn't seem too conspicuous while fighting the urge to linger and appreciate, I had just enough time to catch the tune they were singing to keep time with the swinging and jumping. I recognized it as something familiar, something I had known from somewhere, but since I didn't have time to hear the words and since they were all singing out of breath anyway, I dismissed this unidentified tune and made my way to the more important meeting.

But as the afternoon and the conversation wore on, and I wore out, I caught myself mentally humming the tune I had picked up from the girls. It was familiar and pleasant and something from my past; in spite of everything else going on in the room at that time, that tune kept fighting its way to the front of my consciousness.

Since I can't see my own face at times like these, I have no idea how I must have looked to the others sitting around the table; but there I sat listening as best as I could with one ear and humming that old tune in my heart.

About midafternoon, I began to piece the words in their appropriate places in the tune. At first, I just fitted the words instead of a hum here or there and didn't even think or even remember the connection. But suddenly it came to me and I remembered the song and the circumstances.

Jesus loves the little children,
All the children of the world.
Red and yellow, black and white,
They are precious in His sight,
Jesus loves the little children of the world.

When the words came to me, my memories jumped back to those Sunday School days so many years ago when we sang this song heartily and meant it. At the time in our valley, we didn't know that much about all four colors. We knew about white, but as yet we hadn't had a lot of experience with red, yellow, or black; so when we sang, the emphasis was on the "Jesus loves" and "precious in His sight" parts. But we still meant it, all of it.

In the context of the kind of afternoon I was having, I saw the wisdom of child's play and the songs that go with it. How many problems of this world could be solved if we could just catch a glimpse of the idea that all people are precious in His sight? How many people suffer every day because we don't realize or care that God loves His children in the world? How many times have we been caught in a situation where we just wanted to shout out, "God made us different by design, but He still loves us"?

We develop political systems and idealogies; we

build nations and empires; we direct programs and policies all in order to achieve the reality of the words of a Sunday School song.

That afternoon, I listened to arguments. I interpreted, moderated, mediated, exchanged, translated, and organized. I structured compromises, constructed scenarios, and developed strategies of procedure. But I did all that because I'm not much of a teacher. If I had had the natural teaching gift of Mrs. Smith, I would have found some crayons and some old leftover wallpaper, and I would have taught those people to sing,

> Jesus loves the little children,
> All the children of the world.
> Red and yellow, black and white,
> They are precious in His sight,
> Jesus loves the little children of the world.

If it would have had the same effect on the people at that meeting that Mrs. Smith's song had on me, it would have been more valuable than our arguments and strategies.

The Lesson of
GIVING AN ANSWER

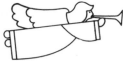

BOBBY MACK PALMER was a strange fellow. We called him strange because he was different from the rest of us. But maybe we were the strange ones and he was normal.

In those days we wouldn't have known what the word "shy" meant, but Bobby Mack was the kind of kid who had to leave the classroom to blow his nose.

Bobby Mack didn't talk much, but he wasn't really quiet. He made noises. In other words, Bobby Mack was the Sunday School Class Special Effects Man.

When we studied the Children of Israel wandering in the wilderness, he sat in his chair staring at Mrs. Murphy, not answering questions, but going, "Klopt—Klopt—Klopt." When we told him he didn't sound like a horse, he explained that those were camels walking in the sand.

When we studied about the shepherds of the Bible, and there were a lot of them, he would make the sounds of sheep baaing.

When we studied about how God made the water

burn, he made the sound of a fire truck.

But the strangest thing he ever did was on the morning that our lesson leaflet was labeled, "Exodus 28:1-14 — Priestly Garments."

Mrs. Murphy picked Bobby Mack to read first, and we listened attentively, not so much because we were interested in what the Word said, but because we were eager to hear what Bobby Mack might add.

He started, "And take thou unto thee Aaron thy brother and his sons with him from among the Children of Israel, that he may minister unto Me in the priest's office, even Aaron . . . , even Aaron . . . , even Aar . . . ," and he paused before he came to Nadab, Abihu, Eleazar, and Ithamar and he got that look on his face that you might get if your father caught you riding the calves out behind the barn. Then he jumped up and ran across the room and crawled under the little table by the door. And no amount of coaxing by Mrs. Murphy or teasing by us could call him out again.

As we walked out the door, Mrs. Murphy said, "Bobby Mack, come out from under that table. Always be prepared to give an answer to everyone who asks you to give the reason for the hope that you have." And Bobby Mack followed us to church.

Pronouncing hard words out loud is always a challenging and demoralizing task even for the boldest. But pronouncing hard Bible words out loud is an especially excruciating endeavor. If you mispronounce them, everybody looks at you as if you're not a good Christian. And they look as though you ought

125

to pray that God won't punish you because you can't say Nadab, Abihu, Eleazar, and Ithamar—the sons of Aaron—or even Jehoiachin. Besides that, regardless of how you say the names, someone will tell you that you said them wrong.

Nevertheless, hiding under the table did seem to be a bit bizarre at the time. But as the years have gone by, and I've had time to reflect on Bobby Mack's behavior as if it were a parable, I've come to realize that I might have been too harsh.

That's a fairly common human response to difficult passages and times. Sometimes I go to great lengths to avoid the people with whom I think I have had a conflict. There have been days when I have retreated into the bathroom to wash my hands fifty times to avoid meeting a colleague. Sometimes I go to great lengths to avoid telling people who don't know me well the most important fact about me.

Not long ago I was speaking to a "secular" group, whoever "secular" people are. It was a large group of about a thousand. When I had finished, someone up near the front asked, so that everybody could hear, "How did you learn to be such an optimist?"

As I stood there in front of those one thousand "secular" people, my first impulse was to run hide under the table like Bobby Mack had done, but I remembered the instruction of the Lord through the mouth of Mrs. Murphy, and I boldly gave an answer or reason for the hope that is within me.

That's what I learned in Sunday School and that's all I really need to know.

The Lesson of
COTTON CHOPPING

SOMETIMES YOU CAN LEARN the lessons of Sunday School even when you're not there.

One day in the beauty of early June, I was chopping cotton. Now, chopping cotton is a rather important activity in the overall theme of feeding and clothing the nation, but it is also an activity fraught with unexcitement. In other words, you walk through the red dust all day and cut weeds away from the cotton plants.

In our high tech era, cotton choppers often minimize the tedium by wearing miniature tape players and headsets. But in the pregadget age, we resorted to other means. For example, if there were several workers in the same field, we could walk alongside a married couple and eavesdrop on their quarreling. That's what I was doing on the day I learned so much.

In the middle of the afternoon, the woman said to the man, "Would you come over in my row and help me cut these big weeds?"

"Dear," the man replied rather good naturedly, "remember what the Bible says, 'God helps those who help themselves.' "

"The Bible doesn't say that," the woman answered curtly. "You're just lazy."

"Does too," the man answered. "I went to Sunday School more than you did when I was a kid. I should know what the Bible says."

"Well, it doesn't say anything like that," the woman responded. And with that vigorous beginning, the argument raged for a full thirty minutes.

Finally, either realizing that he didn't have a case or weary from the debate, the man conceded, but only just a bit. "Well, maybe the Bible doesn't say that. But at least that's what my Sunday School teacher told us."

In this simple cotton field testimony, there seems to be a rather profound message. Some thirty years later, the man remembered the words of his teacher and still thought it was the Gospel.

That's both a promise and a reprimand.

The Lesson of
THE SWEETER DAY

THE GOOD THING about learning songs in Sunday School is that for the rest of your life, they take on the look of the person that you first heard sing them.

I'm sure that you have heard some variation of this little assumption so often that surely you have a defense against it. Someone is always seeing similarities where none exist. The old adage tells us that dogs look like their masters, but I don't believe that. Of course, I only know two dog owners. About the biggest person I know owns a Chihuahua and about the smallest person I know owns a St. Bernard. There's another adage that tells us that cars look like their owners, but about the only people I know who really put much stock in that are teenage girls.

I agree that seeing these kinds of similarities stretches the imagination a bit, but I still maintain that songs can look like the people who sing them. Of course, this isn't true with all songs or all singers. Some songs just seem to be tailor-made for specific people. How often have you heard someone sing a song, and you say to yourself, "That fits"? From then on, anyone else who attempts to sing that song won't quite make it. On the other hand, how often do you see someone who attempts to sing a song that doesn't quite fit?

During opening exercises, Mrs. Henderson didn't sing too much. Mrs. Smith always led, and Mrs. Henderson sat out among the children herding, corralling, and coaxing. But on special days when we sang one special song, Mrs. Smith would step aside for Mrs. Henderson to come up and lead.

And that was so right. It was Mrs. Henderson's song, and everybody knew it. She's the one who taught it to us. She's the one who led us and corrected us if we didn't understand. And she's the one who knew what it meant.

> Every day with Jesus
>   is sweeter than the day before,
> Every day with Jesus
>   I love Him more and more,
> Jesus saves and keeps me,
>   and He's the one I'm waiting for,
> Every day with Jesus
>   is sweeter than the day before.

As she would lead by singing above us from her place in the front, even the restless and the perpetual mischievous would cease their wiggling and gouging and stand still with calmness in body and soul;

130

and the room was filled with a certain quiet, a serene and peaceful kind of quiet rather than a forced or manipulated quiet.

Although "hearty" was the descriptive word for most of our singing, "peaceful" would be appropriate to describe how we participated when Mrs. Henderson sang.

As she would lead by singing above us, we didn't hear the age in her voice or see the trembling in her hands. With our heads partially bowed in a reverence required by the moment, we watched and followed and said to ourselves, "This is so right."

This was Mrs. Henderson's song because it was her life. Mrs. Henderson was everybody's grandmother. She was the kind of lady we all thought we knew better than we really did. The reason for that was not deception but a special kind of caring. We children talked to Mrs. Henderson more than we talked to any other adult in church; and because of that, we thought we knew her; but in reality, in those conversations we talked and she listened.

Frequently she would carry things in the pocket of her dress and would surprise us with some little special gift—a cookie, a special piece of embroidery, or something she carved from a piece of twig. But these gifts were conceived and designed for the specific individual, and a gift from Mrs. Henderson became a prized possession, something that we cherished because it reminded us that some adult really had thought about us.

Mrs. Henderson knew Jesus personally. She was

on a first-name basis with Him. She prayed often and long. She read her Bible thoroughly and deeply, and she waited with great excitement for that day that Jesus would come again.

She was the only Christian I have ever known who spent more time celebrating Easter than celebrating Christmas. She baked special goodies, mailed out announcement cards, and gave us gifts.

Each year we had a children's Christmas play to satisfy the needs of the rest of the church, but we had an Easter play to satisfy Mrs. Henderson.

And each day with Mrs. Henderson was sweeter than the day before because each day she learned to love Jesus more. For her, true excitement was learning something new about Jesus. The Bible was a gold mine of rich nuggets contributing to the plentiful life, and every day she dug and dug until she found that special nugget for the day so that she could love Jesus more. On Sunday, she would describe those nuggets to us with such vividness that we learned to love Him more too.

One day in early June when the sky was luscious and the valley was alive with plants and it was early enough in the summer vacation that we hadn't grown bored yet, I went down to Mrs. Henderson's house to help her hoe her garden.

During the afternoon, we worked together and we talked. Or rather I talked and Mrs. Henderson listened and asked, and I talked more. But then in what seemed to be a moment out of context, she said that it would thrill her if I would sing her a song. I winced and explained to Mrs. Henderson my sore rib syndrome and that my nickname was Off-Key Cliff. She smiled a smile of reassurance instead of ridicule, and told me that she had a song just for me. She would teach it to me and it would be my special song for the rest of my life. I was excited about that possibility, and she was so convincing that for a moment, I actually believed I could do it. I listened, and she sang—the only song I had ever heard her sing.

> Every day with Jesus
>   is sweeter than the day before,
> Every day with Jesus
>   I love Him more and more,
> Jesus saves and keeps me,
>   and He's the one I'm waiting for,
> Every day with Jesus
>   is sweeter than the day before.

When she finished, she pleaded with me to try, but she pleaded with such gentleness and genuineness that I could attempt it without any hint of fear that I might be off key or any hint of the feeling of disloyalty that I had taken her song.

I sang and it felt good. Since my ears are on the side instead of the front, I can't hear myself sing, so I don't know whether it sounded good or not. But it felt good.

When I had finished, Mrs. Henderson had moisture in her eyes and she told me that I had done it beautifully. Then she told me that I should sing that song because it was the song that fit me. And since I believe that songs can fit the people who sing them, and because I had seen her sing the song, I believed her. And I have sung that song every day since. I don't sing out loud nor in crowds. I probably don't even sing on key.

I don't know whether the song fits my voice or not, but I pray that it fits my life the way it fit Mrs. Henderson.

The Lesson of
THE URGENT CHILDREN

WHEN YOU SEE THE WORLD through the eyes of a child, you get one perspective. As you grow older, you get another. There are some who might argue that this is the difference between perception and reality—and that one perspective is more valid than the other. But I don't agree. It seems to me that we need both perspectives; as they combine, they give us a clearer sense of the whole of life.

Now that I'm an adult, I have begun to see new meaning in some of those childhood Sunday School experiences. There is a reason why you sing before you study. There is a reason why one person prays long and the other short. There is a reason why the little children are in the back room.

After having spent terms of service as a teacher in the adult Sunday School department, I have even learned a new function for children. They remind us when to change activities and get serious.

In the church I now attend, the adult class meets upstairs in a room with big windows where the bright

Sunday sun floods in and warms our faces and hearts. We have cushioned comfortable chairs and the carpet is thick. In this environment and with these people, Sunday School is a pleasant place to be. Through the week, I find myself looking forward to the warmth of Sunday morning.

The children meet in the back room of the basement. They don't have big windows, and they don't have cushioned chairs or carpet. But they do have a bell which tells them when to start and when to finish.

Upstairs we don't have a bell. We don't even have a clock. But we don't need it. We have something even more dependable to tell us when class is over — the children. Regardless of the depth of our discussion, regardless of the sincerity of the moment, the adult class ends when the bell rings downstairs and the children come running up armed with smiles on their faces, stored-up energy in their limbs, and today's artwork in their hands. When they come bouncing into the room, we know that class is over and it is time to commence learning in a more serious vein.

It isn't just their presence that interrupts, even when they manage to restrain themselves from barging in or banging on the door. These children interrupt because they bring a new level of energy and urgency into the place. The artwork is more than crayon marks on paper. It always comes with a story, and the story is urgent. It must be retold and retold right now.

136

Some people, and particularly some adult teachers, might find that kind of terminus to a good session somewhat disconcerting. But I don't. In fact, I'm not sure but what it's scriptural.

One day Jesus was holding services. The disciples were on usher duty. When the children came barging in with their stories to tell, the disciples, being the good ushers that they were, said something like, "Shh. You'll have to wait quietly out here in the hall. Jesus is talking seriously about the kingdom."

But that wasn't what Jesus wanted. He said, "Wait a minute. You people have it all wrong. These children are the ones who know about the kingdom. If we don't learn from them, we won't know how to enter it. Let those children come to me, and let's all get serious about this business of learning how to be children of God."

In our class, we follow that little piece of advice every Sunday morning, exactly at ten minutes until eleven. And I know the time even without a clock or bell.

The Lesson of
THE GOOD NEIGHBOR

HOW LONG HAD IT BEEN? Twenty years? Five years? Fourteen years? Six weeks? In my remembering the chronology had been scrambled, and the people and experiences ran together and around each other, jumping into my consciousness in no order or sequence!

But I was going back for Rally Day. Although no one knew it at the time, this would be the last Rally Day ever. This little country congregation, like so many others, was becoming a victim of progress. As more powerful tractors were produced, as farms grew larger and families were more scattered, the children, the people of the next generation, left the valley for careers and fame elsewhere. Eventually the congregation was so small that maintaining a church was not considered sound stewardship.

But this was Rally Day, and there would be a crowd—a crowd of the present but an even bigger crowd of the past and the memories. I was going back. There are those who say you can't go home again, but I've never quite figured out what that means. I go home quite regularly in my memories.

Not only was I going back, but I was taking a crowd—my new loved ones. This was the exciting part. The loved ones and the legends of our youth are an integral part of who we are now, for they have made us and shaped us into what we are and are becoming.

Through the years we adopt and are adopted by our new loved ones—spouses and children.

As they come into our lives *in medias res,* we struggle to find the memories and the words to recount that which has shaped us. Because of our inadequacies with language, we long for the day when we can go back, when the new loved ones can meet the old loved ones and can visualize what was and then believe the legends and the happenings.

The day for joining the past and the present had come. Now my wife and children could put faces to names and curtain walls to places and corners.

Although this was Sunday School, I was going mainly because of the memories—for the reliving and the reunion. It wasn't that I was calloused or too sophisticated to learn; but I had been through it so many years at this place, and so many years at other places so like this place, and I had been through it all in my memories over and over again. I was so focused on the past that I forgot that I might learn something to be used in the future.

I wasn't disappointed. The place was as royal as I had remembered, but smaller. The people were as gracious, and I winced in mock embarrassment when they told my children how I had acted in Sunday School when I was their age.

And the ritual was just as rich. Because there were only a few children, my own and the children of my peers were called up to recite what Bible verses they might know, and we nodded with the joy of tradition when several recited John 3:16. And we laughed out loud with the reality of tradition when some recited, "Jesus wept."

And we all sang the old choruses including "Every day with Jesus," and I worshiped on the predicate.

The Sword Drill was just as fast as it used to be, and the winner licked her fingers just as I remembered Mary Alice doing.

As the ceremony progressed, and I regressed to being a little boy again, I punched my family members at the regular intervals with that knowing punch that says, "See! See what I told you! Now do you believe me?" Or I punched sometimes just to remind them that I already knew what was coming next.

For I did know what was coming next—I had played it all out in my remembering so many times through the years. And now I understood myself a little better—why I hold certain things dear, why I set the objectives I set, and why I read the Bible as I do. There were no surprises—just memories and appreciation.

At the end of the service, the one deacon of memory who was still active in the church stood for the conclusion.

Then I relaxed. The service had been rich. The memories had been refreshing, but it was now time to return to the present — to get back into the world of now.

In a fashion so typical of many churchgoers, I half listened to the concluding remarks while I put away the hymnal, retrieved the children who had crawled under the pew in front of us, and gathered up belongings strewn by our young family.

After all, concluding remarks are only that — semicolons that lead us from then to now.

But Brother Roy, in a voice made strong through the years of shouting at cattle, and in a spirit made genuine through the years of walking with Jesus, said simply, "Become a Christian. It'll make your neighbor a better person." Then he prayed.

Suddenly that last Rally Day took on an entirely new meaning. I had come for the memories of the old lessons, but I went away with the conviction and the blessing of the new one.

I can only pray that I live my life in such a way that it is easier for my neighbor to be a good person.

The Lesson of
SUNDAY SCHOOL

THE SNOW WAS BLOWING; the ice was forming; and the curving country roads had already grown treacherous. We thought of turning back, but even that seemed dangerous; so we drove on ahead telling ourselves that it was of no value because surely no one else would venture out on a morning like this.

Finally, we came over a little hill and spotted our destination, a small country church sitting boldly against the climate. Although we had never been there before, we knew it was the right place. I had been asked to come to speak, and the directions were clear. But even more importantly, we knew this was the right place because it looked so familiar.

To our surprise, the place was full to the point of crowded, and the people inside brought warmth to the church and the day.

After the opening exercise of singing and taking the appropriate offering, the children disappeared behind the closing curtains, and we all began to study.

Standing in front, I tried to get my mouth to speak of adult concerns, but my mind refused and I became a boy again, half expecting The Old Mare to whinny or Mrs. Murphy to call on me to say the books in order. Caught in that tension between past and present, I held class for the requisite period.

When the children came streaming out from behind the curtains and running past me to rejoin their parents in the pews, I knew that class was over, so I moved to a quiet corner where I could reflect.

There I was joined by a man older than I in face and body but, like me, a boy again in memory. He told me of his seventy years in that Sunday School, of the wood stove, and watering tub beneath the tree, of dinner on the grounds, and the Rally Day programs, and of teachers and the Word of God.

He told it all so well that I saw the faces and I heard the words, and I realized that although we had grown up half a country and a generation apart, we were brothers in the Lord and in memory.

Feeling a need to go back to the present but not sure why, I asked him why, after seventy years of being in this Sunday School, he had chosen to risk life and limb to come out on a treacherous morning like this. Surely he had heard all the lessons by now and wasn't expecting anything new.

"Paul told me to come," he told me.

I ran through my mental computer list trying to remember someone named Paul who would have dared recommend me so highly as to bring this man out from his safety.

143

"Paul?" I asked.

With that he took out a worn Bible. At first I thought it might have been something left over from his boyhood days; but as he began to read, I could tell that it wasn't.

"But as for you, continue in what you have learned and have become convinced of because you know those from whom you learned it; and how from infancy you have known the Holy Scriptures, which are able to make you wise for salvation through faith in Christ Jesus." He closed the Bible, looked at me, and said, "My Sunday School taught me that before I even learned to read."

Praise God for all the Mrs. Smiths, Mrs. Murphys, and Mrs. Hendersons of the world who through the Sunday School have always taught us and are still teaching us all we really need to know.